The Contemporary Potter

QUARRY

First published in the United States of America by
Rockport Publishers, Inc.
33 Commercial Street
Gloucester, Massachusetts 01930-5089
Telephone: (978) 282-9590
Facsimile: (978) 283-2742
www.rockpub.com

ISBN 1-56496-699-2

10 9 8 7 6 5 4 3 2 1

Design: Lynn Pulsifer and Bill Dereeza for Spike's
Halo & Sawyer Design Associates, Inc.

Front cover (clockwise from left): Kathy Erteman, p. 81,
Joseph Triplo, p. 144, Jeff Oestreich, p. 241, Geoffrey
Wheeler, p. 115, John Hodge, p. 18

Back cover (clockwise from left): Colby Parsons-O'Keefe,
p. 113, David Calvin Heaps, p. 82, Minako Yamane-Lee,
p. 208, Stan Welsh and Margitta Dietrick, p. 89

Printed in China.

the Contemporary potter

A Collection of the best original work
in earthenware, porcelain, and stoneware

GLOUCESTER MASSACHUSETTS

QUARRY BOOKS

Selected by
Jonathan Fairbanks
Angela Fina
Christopher Gustin

Contents

Earthenware is low-fire pottery made of slightly porous, opaque clay. Red earthenware takes its color from its high iron content. Commercially, earthenware is used to make bricks and tiles.

Earthenware

Susan Sipos Pair of cake stands

Thrown and assembled earthenware

Glaze and Firing: Majolica glaze with
handpainting, oxidation firing
w 10 x h 6 inches
w 25 x h 15 centimeters

Kristin Doner ·············· Red and black amphora ··············
from *Imperial Pinchpot* series
Pinched raku clay

Glaze and Firing: Terra sigillata,
reduction stenciling, glaze, and raku-firing
w 10.5 x h 11 inches
w 27 x h 28 centimeters

Hunt Prothro .... *Red Rim Galactic bowl*

Thrown earthenware

Glaze and Firing: Underglazes, cone
06 oxidation firing in an electric kiln
w 10 x h 10 inches
w 25 x h 25 centimeters

Judith Motzkin .... Spirit Keeper

Thrown and inlaid earthenware

Glaze and Firing: Terra sigillata, and brushed
volatilized salt-glazes, low-fire gas sagger firing
w 20 x h 16 x d 20 inches
w 50 x h 41 x d 50 centimeters

Sheldon Ganstrom .... *Altar with Arch*

Slump-molded, hand-built, assembled,
and epoxied raku clay

Glaze and Firing: Raku glazes and
engobes, raku-firing in an electric kiln
w 20 x h 18 x d 11 inches
w 51 x h 46 x d 28 centimeters

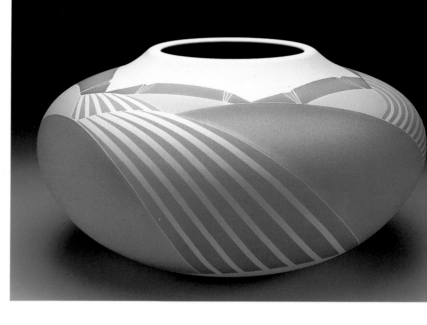

Robert Bede Clarke .... *Ewer* ....

Thrown earthenware

Glaze and Firing: Slips and stains,
sagger firing
w 9.5 x h 16 x d 9.5 inches
w 24 x h 41 x d 24 centimeters

Amy Sarner Williams ..... *Landscape Bowl*
.... *with Striped Fields*

Thrown earthenware

Glaze and Firing: Sprayed vitreous engobes,
cone 06 multi-firing in an electric kiln
w 18 x h 9 x d 18 inches
w 46 x h 23 x d 46 centimeters

Mary Carroll *Jewelled Anemones*

Coil-built, slab-built, and press-molded earthenware

Glaze and Firing: Polychrome glazes and lusters,
cone 03 oxidation firing
w 18 x h 11 x d 18 inches
w 46 x h 28 x d 46 centimeters

Deirdre McCain *Spirit vessel*

Thrown and hand-built raku clay

Glaze and Firing: Brushed copper glaze,
raku-firing and reduction firing
w 13 x h 14 x d 13 inches
w 33 x h 35 x d 33 centimeters

11

Stanley Mace Andersen .... Place setting

Thrown earthenware

> Glaze and Firing: Majolica glaze with
> stains and oxides, cone 03 firing in
> an electric kiln
> Cup h 4 x d 3 inches
> Cup h 10 x d 8 centimeters
> Plate w 11 inches
> Plate w 28 centimeters

Donna McGee .... The Studio

Thrown red earthenware

> Glaze and Firing: Slips and
> transparent glaze with sgraffito,
> gas firing
> w 15 inches
> w 38 centimeters

Sybille Zeldin .... *Fruit server* .....

Hand-built and press-molded
terra cotta

Glaze and Firing: Majolica
glaze, cone 04 firing
w 10 x h 3 x d 21 inches
w 25 x h 8 x d 53 centimeters

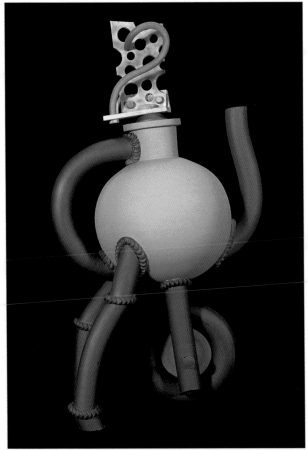

Jake Jacobson .... *Tea-O-Matic 49* ...

Thrown, hand-built, extruded, and
press-molded earthenware

Glaze and Firing: Terra sigillata
and lusters, oxidation multi-firing
w 9 x h 13 x d 7 inches
w 23 x h 33 x d 18 centimeters

13

Susanne G. Stephenson .... *Paint Pots II*

Thrown and adjusted earthenware

Glaze and Firing: Colored slips
and vitreous engobes, cone
03 gas firing
w 10 x h 17.5 x d 9 inches
w 25 x h 44 x d 23 centimeters

Malcolm E. Kucharski .... Vessel

Thrown and hand-built earthenware

Glaze and Firing: Terra sigillata and
oxides, gas firing in an updraft kiln
h 13 x d 15 inches
h 33 x d 38 centimeters

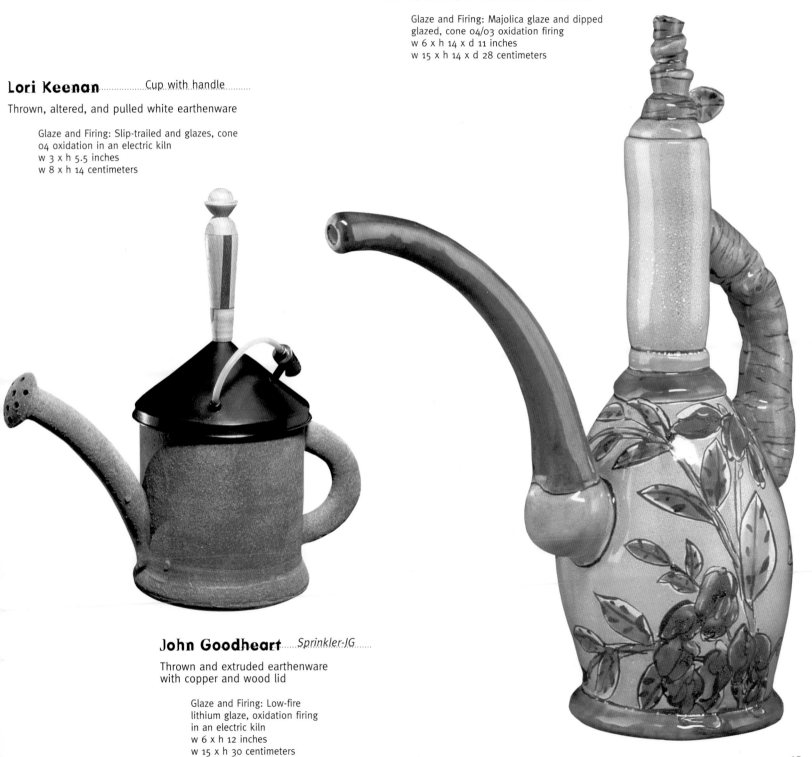

Linda Arbuckle  *T-Pot: Spring in Mardi Gras Colors*

Thrown, altered, and assembled terra cotta

Glaze and Firing: Majolica glaze and dipped glazed, cone 04/03 oxidation firing
w 6 x h 14 x d 11 inches
w 15 x h 14 x d 28 centimeters

Lori Keenan........... *Cup with handle*

Thrown, altered, and pulled white earthenware

Glaze and Firing: Slip-trailed and glazes, cone 04 oxidation in an electric kiln
w 3 x h 5.5 inches
w 8 x h 14 centimeters

John Goodheart.... *Sprinkler-JG*

Thrown and extruded earthenware with copper and wood lid

Glaze and Firing: Low-fire lithium glaze, oxidation firing in an electric kiln
w 6 x h 12 inches
w 15 x h 30 centimeters

Nancy Gardner........Teapot....

Pinched and coil-built terra cotta

Glaze and Firing: White slip,
brushed underglazes, and clear
glaze, cone 04 multi-firing in
an electric kiln
w 8 x h 3 x d 2 inches
w 20 x h 8 x d 5 centimeters

Susan Bostwick........*Finches and Coneflowers*..........

Thrown earthenware

Glaze and Firing: Slips, underglazes,
and brushed glazes, oxidation firing
h 9 x d 6 inches
h 23 x d 15 centimeters

Patrick L. Dougherty *Specter vase*

Thrown white earthenware

Glaze and Firing: Brushed underglazes,
vitreous engobes, and clear glaze,
oxidation firing
w 7 x h 23 inches
w 18 x h 55 centimeters

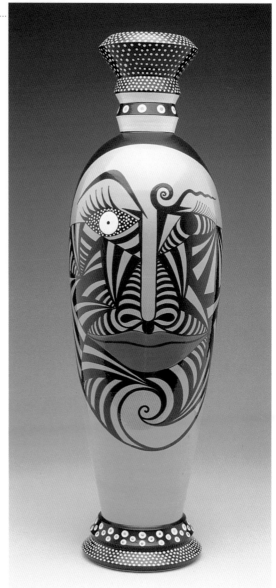

James Lawton Teapot

Thrown and altered earthenware

Glaze and Firing: Terra sigillatta
and glaze, oxidation sagger
firing in a gas kiln
w 12 x h 13 x d 6 inches
w 31 x h 33 x d 15 centimeters

17

David Calvin Heaps .... *Turning Vessel II* ....

Hand-built and slip-cast earthenware, talc, and ball clay

Glaze and Firing: Mat blue glaze,
cone 04 oxidation firing
w 18 x h 10 x d 9 inches
w 46 x h 25 x d 23 centimeters

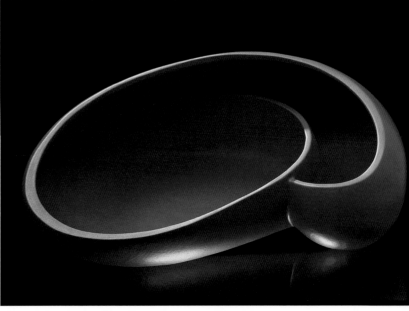

Greg Payce .... Vase grouping ....

Thrown earthenware with hand-built handles

Glaze and Firing: Terra sigillata,
cone 04 oxidation firing in an
electric kiln
w 8 x h 31 x d 6 inches
w 20 x h 78 x d 15 centimeters

Robert L. Wood .... *Sign of the Times* vessel ....

Slab-built, press-molded, and texturized earthenware

Glaze and Firing: Iron oxide wash, cone
3 reduction firing
w 22 x h 20 x d 6 inches
w 55 x h 50 x d 15 centimeters

Deborah Kate Groover................._Glory Restored_

Thrown, altered, and hand-built earthenware

Glaze and Firing: Layered majolica
glazes and stains, cone 04 firing in
an electric kiln
w 12 x h 10 x d 6 inches
w 31 x h 25 x d 15 centimeters

John Hodge................._Studded Bowl_.......

Thrown earthenware

Glaze and Firing: Brushed and
acid-washed, bisque firing
with an electric kiln
w 14 x h 7 x d 14 inches
w 36 x h 18 x d 36 centimeters

Marilee Hall................Cone teapot.................

Cast, hand-built, and carved earthenware

Glaze and Firing: Glazes and stains,
low-fire oxidation firing
w 9 x h 12 inches
w 23 x h 31 centimeters

Kreg Richard Owens...........*Stack* sugar bowl and creamer....

Thrown and hand-built terra cotta

Glaze and Firing: Black and turquoise
gloss glaze interior, terra sigillata
exterior, cone 04 firing
w 5 x h 14 x d 5 inches
w 13 x h 43 x d 13 centimeters

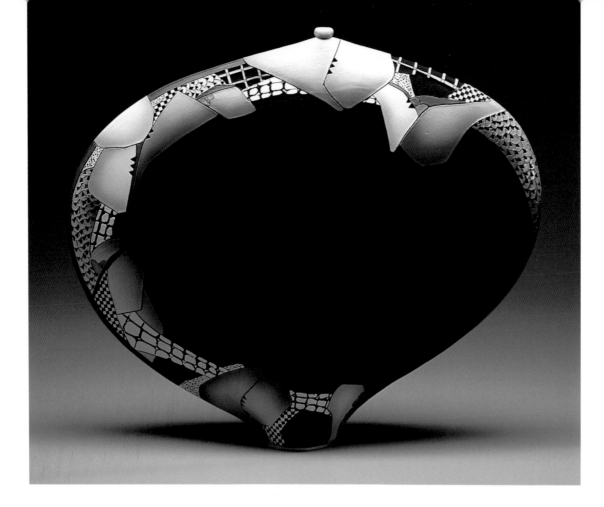

Nancy April .... *Asymmetrical Elliptic Ovi* ......

Hand-built and slump-molded earthenware

Glaze and Firing: Airbrushed and
hand-painted latex glaze amd black
glaze, oxidation multi-firing
w 22 x h 18 x d 6 inches
w 56 x h 46 x d 15 centimeters

Jill Bonovitz .... *Sage* ....

Hand-built earthenware

Glaze and Firing: Terra sigillata
and slips, firing in an electric kiln
w 25 x h 4 inches
w 64 x h 10 centimeters

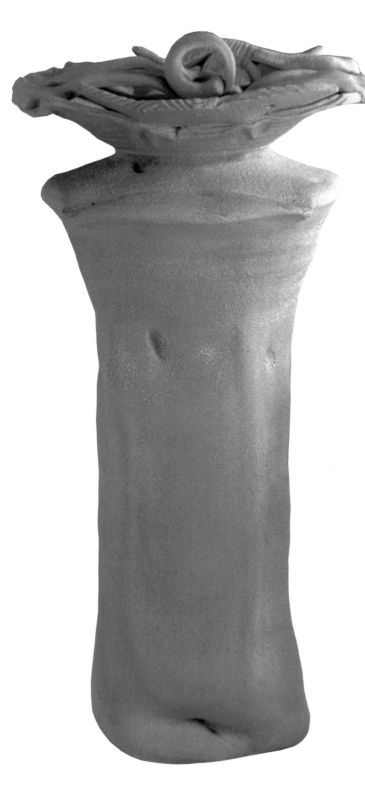

Tom Latka .... *Yes* ....

Extruded and altered earthenware

Glaze and Firing: Reticulating glaze,
cone 01 firing in an electric kiln
w 8 x h 16 x d 4 inches
w 20 x h 41 x d 10 centimeters

Anna Calluori Holcombe .... *Tondo XXIX* ....

Slab-built earthenware

Glaze and Firing: Terra sigillata,
firing in an electric kiln
w 18 x d 3 inches
w 46 x d 8 centimeters

Elaine Alt  *Jester* teapot

Thrown and hand-built earthenware

Glaze and Firing: Underglazes, mat glaze, gloss glaze, and gold luster with wax resists, multi-firing in an electric kiln
w 12 x h 18 x d 7 inches
w 31 x h 46 x d 18 centimeters

Randy Miseph *Vessel*

Thrown and altered earthenware

Glaze and Firing: Glazes and lusters, oxidation multi-firing
h 7.5 x d 10 inches
h 19 x d 25 centimeters

Don Jones ⋯⋯⋯⋯ *Atmosphere—Turquoise Sunset* ⋯⋯⋯

Thrown white earthenware

Glaze and Firing: Airbrushed underglaze,
brushed clear overglaze, cone 05
oxidation firing in an electric kiln
h 14 x d 15 inches
h 36 x d 38 centimeters

Henry Cavanagh ⋯⋯⋯⋯⋯ *Mom's Diner* cookie jar ⋯⋯⋯

Slip-cast and altered earthenware

Glaze and Firing: Brushed stains, underglazes,
and platinum china paint with decals, cone 04,
cone 06, cone 02, and cone 18 multi-firing
w 7 x h 9 x d 12 inches
w 18 x h 23 x d 34 centimeters

Bill Stewart .... *Trinity* ....

Hand-built and cast earthenware

Glaze and Firing: Glaze, slip,
and grog/glaze mixture, cone
05 oxidation firing
w 25 x h 23 x d 14 inches
w 64 x h 58 x d 36 centimeters

Colleen Zufelt .... Architectural teapot ....

Cast, slab-built, and extruded earthenware

Glaze and Firing: Unglazed, airbrushed
paints and pencil, cone 04 firing in an
electric kiln
w 10 x h 15 x d 8 inches
w 25 x h 38 x d 20 centimeters

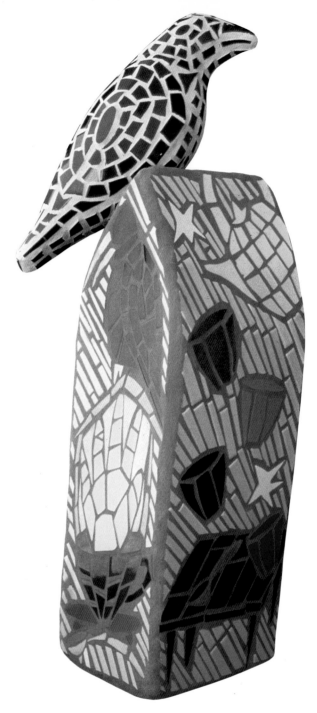

Roberta Kaserman ⋯⋯⋯ *Nesting Instinct* ⋯⋯⋯

Slab-built and press-molded earthenware

Glaze and Firing: Unglazed surface covered
with ceramic mosaic tiles and grouted
w 11 x h 25 x d 8 inches
w 28 x h 64 x d 20 centimeters

Lisa Mandelkern ⋯⋯⋯⋯⋯ Teapot ⋯⋯⋯

Hand-built white earthenware

Glaze and Firing: Brushed low-fire glazes
and underglazes, firing in electric kiln
w 7.5 x h 9.5 x d 4 inches
w 19 x h 24 x d 10 centimeters

Tom Neugebauer......................Windswept......

Thrown raku clay

Glaze and Firing: Rubbed stains and
sprayed copper sulfate, pit-firing
w 17 x h 34 x d 12 inches
w 43 x h 86 x d 31 centimeters

Susan Bostwick......The Grapes Were Few.....

Thrown white earthenware

Glaze and Firing: Brushed slips,
underglazes, and glazes, oxidation firing
h 10 x d 7 inches
h 25 x d 18 centimeters

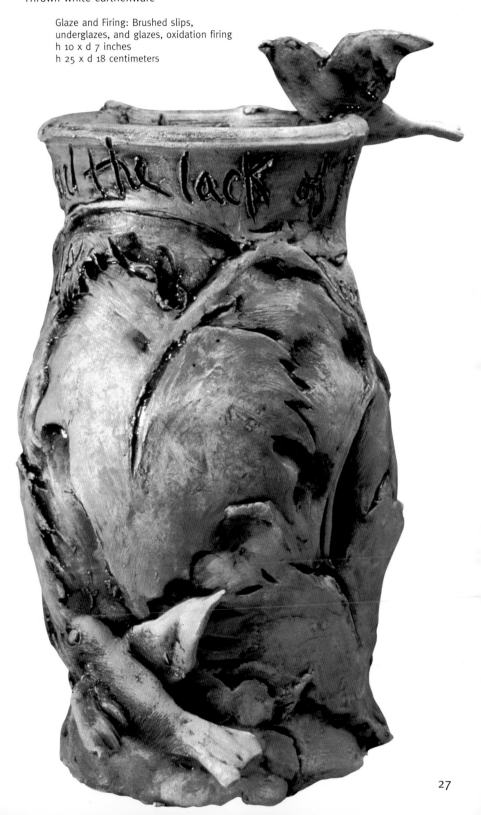

27

Sandra Luehrsen .... *Prickly Heart vessel*

Coil-built and carved terra cotta

Glaze and Firing: Colored slips and glazes,
cone 06 firing in an electric kiln
w 8 x h 14 x d 5 inches
w 21 x h 36 x d 13 centimeters

Piero Fenci .... *Shaker Hatbox*

Hand-built raku clay

Glaze and Firing: Raku glazes, raku-firing
w 17 x h 9 x d 9 inches
w 43 x h 23 x d 23 centimeters

Scott Tubby········· Vessel·····

Thrown, trimmed, and sanded earthenware

Glaze and Firing: Unglazed, polished,
gas sagger firing
w 9 x h 8.5 inches
w 23 x h 22 centimeters

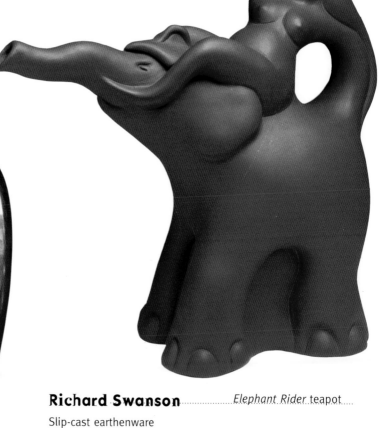

Richard Swanson················· *Elephant Rider* teapot····

Slip-cast earthenware

Glaze and Firing: Unglazed, cone 5
multi-firing in an electric kiln
w 11.5 x h 11.5 x d 5.5 inches
w 29 x h 29 x d 14 centimeters

Lynn Duryea .... *Earth Vessel III* ....

Hand-built and slab-built earthenware

Glaze and Firing: Slips and crusty glazes,
oxidation firing in an electric kiln
w 13 x h 25 x d 13 inches
w 33 x h 64 x d 33 centimeters

Woody Hughes .... Ewer and tray set ......

Thrown and altered terra cotta

Glaze and Firing: Terra sigillata,
oxidation firing in an electric kiln
w 19 x h 11 x d 8 inches
w 48 x h 28 x d 20 centimeters

Mark Johnson .... Pouring vessel ....

Thrown and altered earthenware

Glaze and Firing: Glaze and terra sigillata,
cone 04 firing in an electric kiln
w 14 x h 16 x d 10 inches
w 36 x h 41 x d 25 centimeters

Ann Gabhart .... Bowl ....

Thrown terra cotta

Glaze and Firing: Slips and glaze,
cone 04 firing in an electric kiln
w 11.5 x h 7 x d 11.5 inches
w 29 x h 17 x d 29 centimeters

Robert Edward Carlson......Vessel......

Thrown, extruded, and hand-built raku clay

Glaze and Firing: Raku glazes, acrylics,
and applied 23-karat gold and silver
leaf, raku-firing
w 10 x h 24 inches
w 25 x h 61 centimeters

Abby Huntoon......Vase with plane......

Press-molded earthenware

Photo by Tom McPherson
Glaze and Firing: Low-fire glazes and
underglazes, cone 04 firing in an electric kiln
w 22 x h 20.5 x d 14 inches
w 56 x h 52 x d 36 centimeters

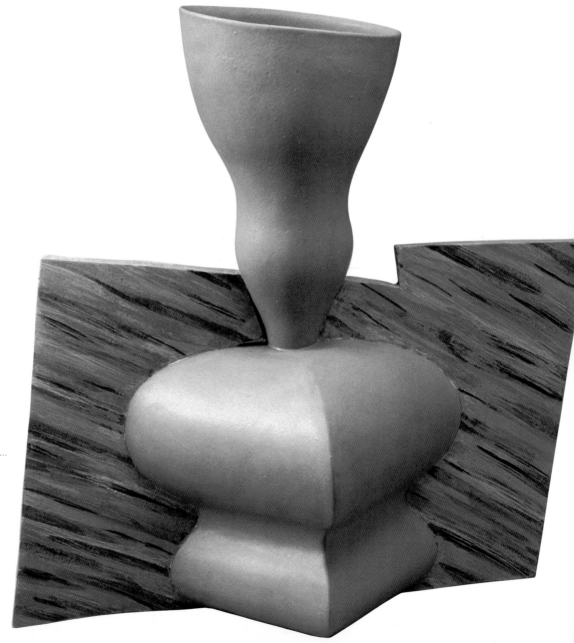

Holly Walker ·················· Teapot ······

Hand-built terra cotta

Glaze and Firing: Slip, glaze, and stains,
firing in an electric kiln
w 8 x h 9 x d 6 inches
w 20 x h 23 x d 15 centimeters

Mark Tomczak ·········· Teapot ····

Thrown and altered earthenware

Glaze and Firing: Terra sigillata,
firing in an electric kiln
w 8.5 x h 6.5 x d 4.5 inches
w 22 x h 17 x d 11 centimeters

Abby Huntoon ··············· *Island* ···········

Slab-built, coil-built, extruded, and
press-molded earthenware

Photo by Mark Foose
Glaze and Firing: Low-fire glazes,
cone 04 firing in an electric kiln
w 11 x h 20 x d 11 inches
w 28 x h 50 x d 28 centimeters

Rosalie Wynkoop .... *Bouquet plate* ....

Thrown and slump-molded earthenware

Glaze and Firing: Majolica glaze over
black slip, cone 04 firing in an electric kiln
w 20 x h 20 inches
w 50 x h 50 centimeters

Melissa Greene ...... *Idluk: Fabulous Fish* .....

Thrown white earthenware

Glaze and Firing: Terra sigillata,
burnished, with wax-resist, bisque-firing
and smoked
w 16 x h 16 inches
w 41 x h 41 centimeters

Sally Porter .... *Teapot with double handle* ....

Hand-built earthenware

Glaze and Firing: Vitreous engobes,
oxidation firing
w 12 x h 15 x d 6 inches
w 30 x h 43 x d 15 centimeters

Kevin A. Myers ..... *Totemic Tea #2*

Thrown, altered, and hand-built earthenware

Glaze and Firing: Cone 06 clear crackle glaze over brushed black slip with china paint, gold luster, and sgraffito, cone 06 oxidation multi-firing
w 14.5 x h 49 x d 15 inches
w 37 x h 125 x d 38 centimeters

James C. Watkins ..... *Ritual Display*

Thrown and hand-built raku clay

Glaze and Firing: Raku copper glaze, raku-firing
w 9 x h 12 inches
w 23 x h 31 centimeters

Judith Salomon ..... *Green Envelope vase*

Slip-cast earthenware

Glaze and Firing: Low-fire glazes, cone 4 firing in an electric kiln
w 24 x h 13 x d 11 inches
w 61 x h 33 x d 28 centimeters

Claudia Reese .... *Lemon and Pepper* platter ..

Press-molded and assembled earthenware

Glaze and Firing: Colored slip and clear
glaze with sgraffito, cone 04 firing in an
electric kiln
w 18 inches
w 46 centimeters

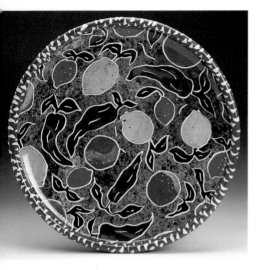

Lori Mills .... Cup and saucer ....

Thrown and altered earthenware

Glaze and Firing: Colored slips
and glazes, low-fire oxidation firing
w 6 x h 5.5 x d 6 inches
w 15 x h 14 x d 15 centimeters

Lori Mills .... Tiered tulip holder ......

Thrown, altered, and assembled earthenware

Glaze and Firing: Colored slips and glazes,
low-fire oxidation firing
w 13.5 x h 26 x d 5.5 inches
w 34 x h 66 x d 14 centimeters

John Ground .... *Ritual* jar ....

Hand-built terra cotta texturized with
burned-out ground corn cobs

Glaze and Firing: Glaze, firing in an
electric kiln
w 13 x h 28 x d 7 inches
w 33 x h 71 x d 18 centimeters

Wesley Anderegg .... Cups and saucers

Pinched, carved, and assembled earthenware

Glaze and Firing: Slips and glazes, firing in an
electric kiln
w 6 x h 6 x d 4 inches
w 15 x h 15 x d 10 centimeters

Mary Kelton Seyfarth ..... *Mediterranean* cup ...

Thrown terra cotta

Glaze and Firing: Soda-blue glazed interior,
cone 02 firing in an electric kiln
w 10 x h 5 x d 10 inches
w 25 x h 13 x d 25 centimeters

Jonathan Kaplan ....Footed tea set.......

Slip-cast and assembled terra cotta

Glaze and Firing: Airbrushed and sprayed
underglazes, glaze, and brushed metallic
pigments, cone 3 oxidation firing
w 8 x h 10 inches
w 20 x h 25 centimeters

Jane Dillon ....Jar, cup, and tray.....

Thrown, hand-built, altered, and assembled
earthenware

Glaze and Firing: Slips, glazes, and terra
sigillata, cone 04 oxidation firing
w 24 x h 16 x d 11 inches
w 60 x h 40 x d 28 centimeters

Paul and Claudette Gerhold .... *Palms vessel*

Thrown raku clay with kyanite

Glaze and Firing: Raku glazes, silver, tin, and
copper glazes, burnished, raku-firing in an electric kiln,
and reduction firing
w 20 x h 25 x d 20 inches
w 51 x h 64 x d 51 centimeters

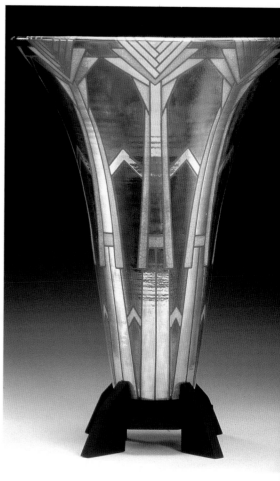

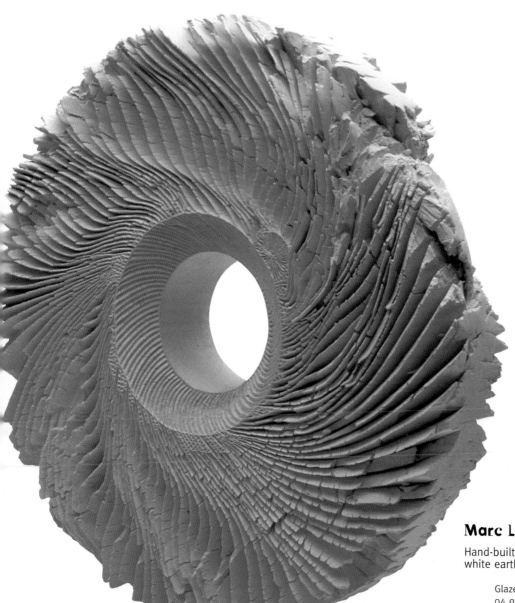

Marc Leuthold .... *White Wheel*

Hand-built, trimmed, and carved
white earthenware

Glaze and Firing: Unglazed, cone
04 oxidation firing
w 10 x h 10 x d 3 inches
w 25 x h 25 x d 8 centimeters

George McCauley Teapot

Thrown and altered earthenware

Glaze and Firing: Terra sigillata,
iron wash, and glaze, cone 02 soda-firing
w 9 x h 11.5 inches
w 23 x h 30 centimeters

Judy Kogod Colwell *Fish and Rice Bowl* platter

Thrown red earthenware

Glaze and Firing: Slip-trailed, brushed colored
stains, underglaze, and clear glaze, cone 04
in an electric kiln
w 19 x h 5 inches
w 48 x h 13 centimeters

Gina Bobrowski and Triesch Voelker *Teapot*

Thrown and hand-built terra cotta

Glaze and Firing: Majolica glaze, cone 04 firing
in an electric kiln
w 10 x h 6 x d 4 inches
w 25 x h 15 x d 10 centimeters

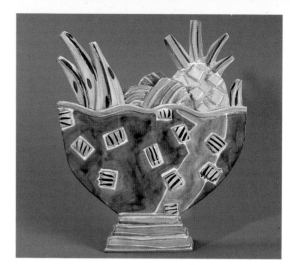

Sara Post Centerpiece

Slab-built earthenware

Glaze and Firing: Majolica glaze,
cone 3 firing in an electric kiln
w 15 x h 22 x d 3 inches
w 45 x h 66 x d 9 centimeters

Ingrid Lilligren *Transference*

Thrown, altered, and embossed earthenware

Glaze and Firing: Cone 04 lithium mat glazes,
multi-firings in an electric kiln
w 13 x h 8 x d 7 inches
w 33 x h 20 x d 18 centimeters

Jonathan Kaplan Single glass tripod

Slip-cast terra cotta

Glaze and Firing: Airbrushed and sprayed
underglaze, glaze, and brushed metallic
pigments, cone 3 oxidation firing
h 16 x d 13 inches
h 41 x d 33 centimeters

Jennie Bireline.......*Blue Target Origami vessel*...

Slab-built earthenware

Glaze and Firing: Terra sigillata and burnished
gold leaf, cone 04 gas firing
w 20 x h 25.5 x d 6 inches
w 51 x h 65 x d 15 centimeters

Judith Schumacher.................*Hemisphere*...

Press-molded and hand-built white earthenware

Glaze and Firing: Gloss white glaze over mat
black glaze, cone 06 oxidation firing
w 9.5 x h 6 inches
w 24 x h 13 centimeters

Kevin Donohue.......*Covered jar*.......

Thrown earthenware

Glaze and Firing: Majolica glaze, Mason
stains, and overglaze enamels, cone 07
oxidation firing in an electric kiln
w 3.5 x h 7 inches
w 9 x h 18 centimeters

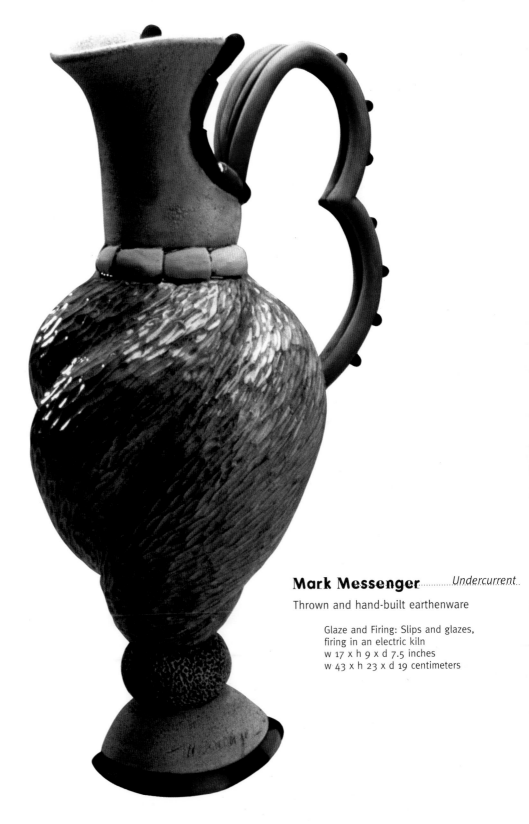

Mark Messenger .... *Undercurrent*

Thrown and hand-built earthenware

Glaze and Firing: Slips and glazes,
firing in an electric kiln
w 17 x h 9 x d 7.5 inches
w 43 x h 23 x d 19 centimeters

Sachiko Kawamura .... *Double Image* ...

Slab-built and inlaid earthenware

Glaze and Firing: Mat white glaze,
cone 9 firing in an electric kiln
w 19 x h 2 inches
w 48 x h 5 centimeters

Hwang Jeng-Daw .... *Dancing*

Slab-built earthenware

Glaze and Firing: Colored glazes,
cone 9 firing in an electric kiln
w 8 x h 4.5 inches
w 19 x h 11 centimeters

Joy Hanken .... Teapot ....

Coil-built terra cotta

Glaze and Firing: Slips, underglazes,
and glazes, cone 06/05 firing
w 8.5 x h 9 x d 3 inches
w 22 x h 23 x d 8 centimeters

Hwang Jeng-Daw .... *A Broken Stone*

Slab-built earthenware

Glaze and Firing: Black slip, cone 9
firing in an electric kiln
w 8 x h 46 inches
w 20 x h 18 centimeters

Katrina Chaytor-Rozman .... *Scroll Pot*

Hand-built earthenware

Glaze and Firing: Slips and glazes, oxidation
firing in an electric kiln
w 18 x h 10 x d 9 inches
w 46 x h 25 x d 23 centimeters

Robert Flynn .... Vase ....

Press-molded, assembled, and altered terra cotta

Glaze and Firing: Low-fire lead glaze, gas firing
with salt and borax
w 9.5 x h 24 x d 6 inches
w 24 x h 24 x d 15 centimeters

Wendy Walgate ......*Vase with Yellow Disks* ......

Hand-built white earthenware

Glaze and Firing: Low-fire multi-glazes,
cone 03 multi-fired in an electric kiln
w 17 x h 27 x d 17 inches
w 43 x h 68 x d 43 centimeters

Richard Milette ·····················*Hydria 13-4165 with Hate*

Press-molded, hand-built, and thrown red earthenware

Glaze and Firing: Glazes and enamels,
oxidation firing in an electric kiln
w 16 x h 16 x d 12 inches
w 41 x h 41 x d 31 centimeters

Paul Rozman ···············*Coffee pot*·····

Thrown earthenware

Glaze and Firing: Majolica glaze and stain
washes, cone 2 oxidation firing
w 9.5 x h 10 x d 3.5 inches
w 24 x h 25 x d 9 centimeters

Carol and Richard Selfridge .... *Leda and the Swan* teapot

Press-molded, thrown, and constructed earthenware

Glaze and Firing: Majolica glaze, cone 04
oxidation firing
w 19 x h 19 x d 4 inches
w 48 x h 48 x d 11 centimeters

Carol and Richard Selfridge .... *Mixed Floral Bouquet in Ming Vase* Plate

Press-molded, thrown, and altered earthenware

Glaze and Firing: Majolica glaze, cone
04 oxidation firing
w 21 x h 3.5 inches
w 53 x h 9 centimeters

Angelo di Petta .... *Allegorical Landscape #21*

Hand-built earthenware

Glaze and Firing: Brown slip, terra sigillata,
and glazes, multi-firing in electric kiln
w 8 x h 3 x d 5 inches
w 20 x h 8 x d 13 centimeters

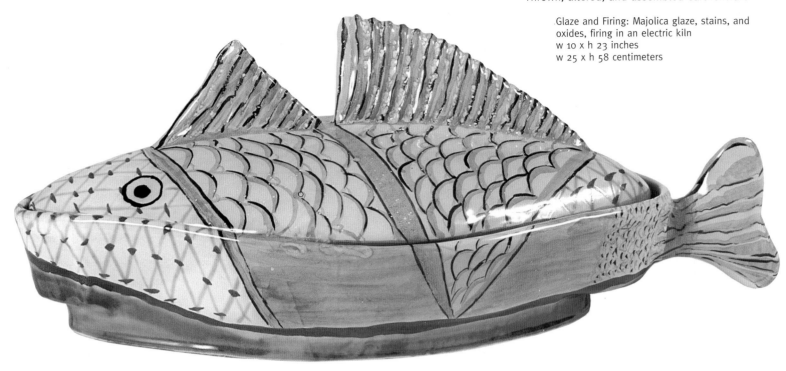

Pat Harvey................................*Fish Dish*..........

Thrown, altered, and assembled earthenware

Glaze and Firing: Majolica glaze, stains, and
oxides, firing in an electric kiln
w 10 x h 23 inches
w 25 x h 58 centimeters

John Kuczwal..............*Fish and the Moon*........

Thrown and press-molded earthenware

Glaze and Firing: Lusters and tin glaze,
oxidation and reduction wood-firing
w 14 x h 6 inches
w 36 x h 15 centimeters

Douglas Baldwin .... *Advanced Throwing*

Hand-built and thrown white earthenware

Glaze and Firing: Unglazed, cone 04
oxidation firing
w 43 x h 7 x d 4.5 inches each
w 109 x h 18 x d 12 centimeters each

Robert Piepenburg .... *Vessel* ....

Thrown and altered fireclay with kyanite

Glaze and Firing: Dipped glaze, reduction raku-firing
w 6 x h 11 inches
w 15 x 28 centimeters

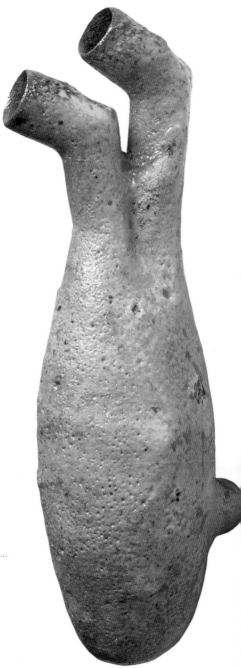

James Shrosbree .... *Django (Humm)* ....

Hand-built earthenware

Glaze and Firing: Low-fire glaze with
sand and slip, gas reduction and electric
oxidation multi-firing
w 2.5 x h 8 x d 3.5 inches
w 6 x h 20 x d 9 centimeters

LANEY K. OXMAN
High Tea

Thrown and hand-built earthenware
Glaze and Firing: Underglaze pencils and stains,
glazes, enamel decals, 24-karat gold, multi-firing

h 36 x d 30 inches
h 91 x d 76 centimeters

SARA E. BRESSEM
Viennese Emperor

Hand-built earthenware
Glaze and Firing: Underglaze, oxides, cone 04
glazes, multi-firing in an electric kiln

w 6 × h 15 × d 4.5 inches
w 15 × h 38 × d 11 centimeters

UNA MJURKA
Untitled

Hand-built earthenware
Glaze and Firing: Underglazes, glaze,
low-fire oxidation firing

h 16-20 inches
h 41-51 centimeters

53

JAMES C. WATKINS
Knight/Night Bird

Thrown and hand-built earthenware
Glaze and Firing: Unglazed, terra sigillata, raku
glaze, sagger firing

w 28 × h 19 inches
w 71 × h 48 centimeters

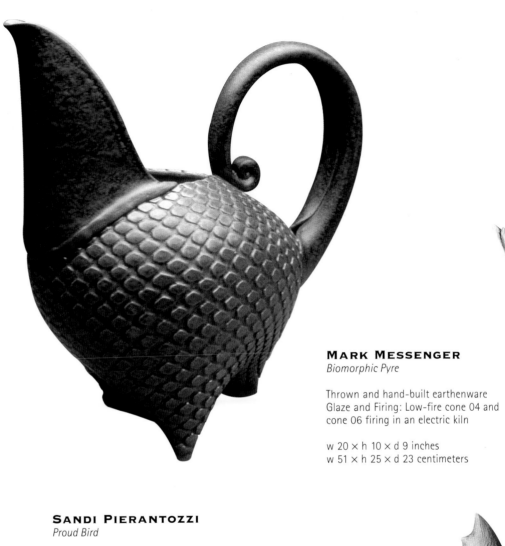

MARK MESSENGER
Biomorphic Pyre

Thrown and hand-built earthenware
Glaze and Firing: Low-fire cone 04 and
cone 06 firing in an electric kiln

w 20 × h 10 × d 9 inches
w 51 × h 25 × d 23 centimeters

SANDI PIERANTOZZI
Proud Bird

Slab-built earthenware
Glaze and Firing: Low-fire glaze, cone 04
bisque/cone 05 glaze, firing in an electric kiln

w 7 × h 8 × d 6 inches
w 18 × h 20 × d 15 centimeters

FARRADAY NEWSOME SREDL
Platter with Fruit and Seashells

Slab-formed earthenware with attached press-molded elements
Glaze and Firing: Brushed cone 05 glazes, firing in an electric kiln

w 25 × h 6 × d 25 inches
w 64 × h 15 × d 64 centimeters

HENRY CAVANAGH
Checker cab cookie jar

Slip-cast earthenware altered from original mold
Glaze and Firing: Stains, glazes, cone 04 bisque, cone 06 glaze, cone 019 luster firing

w 14 × h 9.5 × d 9 inches
w 36 × h 24 × d 23 centimeters

JUDITH SALOMON
Platter

Hand-built earthenware
Glaze and Firing: Cone 04 low-fire
oxidation firing in an electric kiln

w 20 × h 3 inches
w 51 × h 8 centimeters

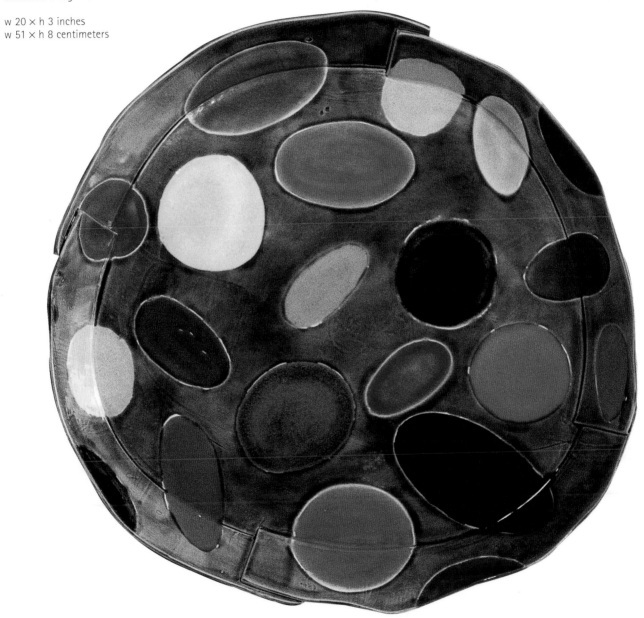

STANLEY MACE ANDERSEN
Tureen

Thrown and hand-built earthenware
Glaze and Firing: Opaque white glaze, brushed
stains and oxides, cone 03 oxidation firing in an
electric kiln

h 10.5 × d 12 inches
h 27 × d 30 centimeters

POSEY BACOPOULOS
Creamer and sugar set

Thrown, altered, and assembled earthenware
Glaze and Firing: Majolica glaze, stains,
cone 04 firing in an electric kiln

w 12 × h 5 × d 9.5 inches
w 30 × h 13 × d 24 centimeters

ANNA CALLOURI HOLCOMBE
Still Life Box VI

Hand-built earthenware
Glaze and Firing: Terra sigillata, underglazes,
low-fire glaze, cone 04 firing in an electric kiln

w 11 × h 21 × d 4 inches
w 28 × h 53 × d 10 centimeters

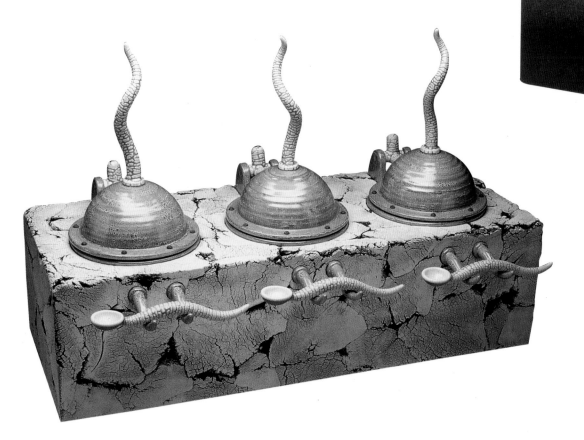

ERIC VAN EIMEREN
Ketchup-Mustard-Pickle-Relish

Press-molded, slip-cast, and hand-built
earthenware
Glaze and Firing: Cone 04 and cone
020 luster, oxidation firing

w 20.5 × h 14 × d 10.5 inches
w 52 × h 36 × d 27 centimeters

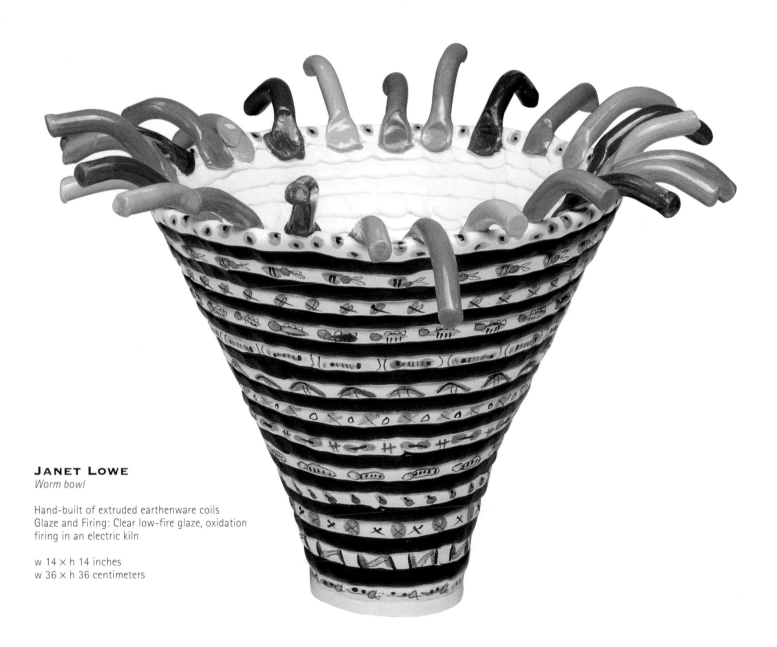

JANET LOWE
Worm bowl

Hand-built of extruded earthenware coils
Glaze and Firing: Clear low-fire glaze, oxidation
firing in an electric kiln

w 14 × h 14 inches
w 36 × h 36 centimeters

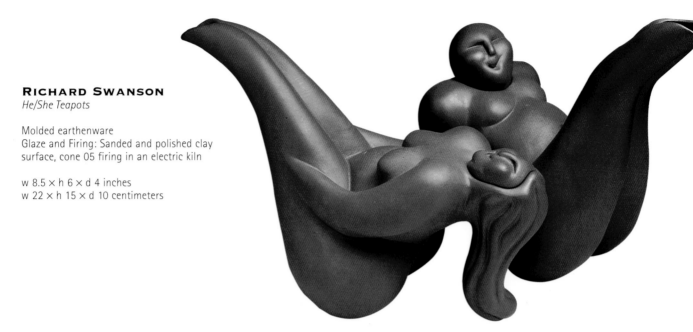

RICHARD SWANSON
He/She Teapots

Molded earthenware
Glaze and Firing: Sanded and polished clay surface, cone 05 firing in an electric kiln

w 8.5 × h 6 × d 4 inches
w 22 × h 15 × d 10 centimeters

JUDY MOTZKIN
Spirit keeper with woven lid

Thrown earthenware with woven coil inlay
Glaze and Firing: Unglazed, terra sigillata polished, and flame-painted with volatized salts, metals, and combustibles, cone 06 gas sagger firing

w 9 × h 9 × d 9 inches
w 23 × h 23 × d 23 centimeters

ROBERT L. WOOD
Paramphoric

Thrown and press-molded earthenware
Glaze and Firing: Stain and frit coloring, cone 01
firing in an electric kiln

w 32 × h 18 × d 14 inches
w 81 × h 46 × d 36 centimeters

BOB DIXON
Covered urn

Thrown and hand-built earthenware
Glaze and Firing: Majolica glaze, oxidation firing

w 20 × h 22 × d 22 inches
w 51 × h 56 × d 56 centimeters

63

TED VOGEL
Black Stack Roost

Hand-built, carved, and press-molded
earthenware
Glaze and Firing: Copper and black mason
stain slip, cone 03 firing in an electric kiln

w 12 × h 21 × d 12 inches
w 30 × h 53 × d 30 centimeters

HARVEY SADOW
Jupiter Diary series

Thrown and hyperextended earthenware
Glaze and Firing: Eutectic slips/siliceous
lacquers, multiple-raku firings

w 10.5 × h 13.5 × d 13.5 inches
w 27 × h 34 × d 34 centimeters

LINDA ARBUCKLE
Bowl: Berries

Thrown earthenware
Glaze and Firing: Majolica glazes,
oxidation firing in an electric kiln

h 2.5 × d 10 inches
h 6 × d 25 centimeters

NANCY GARDNER
Vase

Pinched and coil-built earthenware
Glaze and Firing: Underglazes, clear glaze,
cone 06 oxidation firing

w 18 × h 12 × d 5 inches
w 46 × h 30 × d 13 centimeters

FRANCINE OZEREKO
Still life

Press-molded earthenware
Glaze and Firing: Hand-painted, glazes, cone 04
firing in an electric kiln

w 14 × h 22 × d 2 inches
w 36 × h 56 × d 5 centimeters

**ELISE SHERIDAN
ARNOLD**
Dead Pony

Hand-built earthenware
Glaze and Firing: Cone 06 glaze,
firing in an electric kiln

w 4 × h 14.5 inches
w 10 × h 37 centimeters

DAVID CALVIN HEAPS
Tear drop flasks with stoppers

Slip-cast earthenware
Glaze and Firing: White, black, and jade
glazes, oxidation firing at 300° F
per hour

w 9 × h 6 × d 4.5 inches
w 23 × h 15 × d 11 centimeters

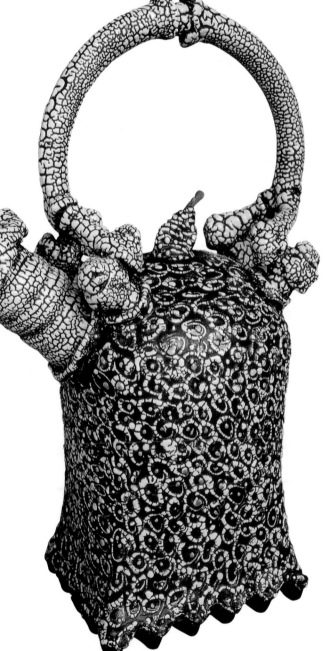

YOSHIRO IKEDA
Teapot

Hand-built earthenware
Glaze and Firing: Manganese glaze,
cone 02-03 oxidation firing

w 14 × h 23 × d 8 inches
w 36 × h 58 × d 20 centimeters

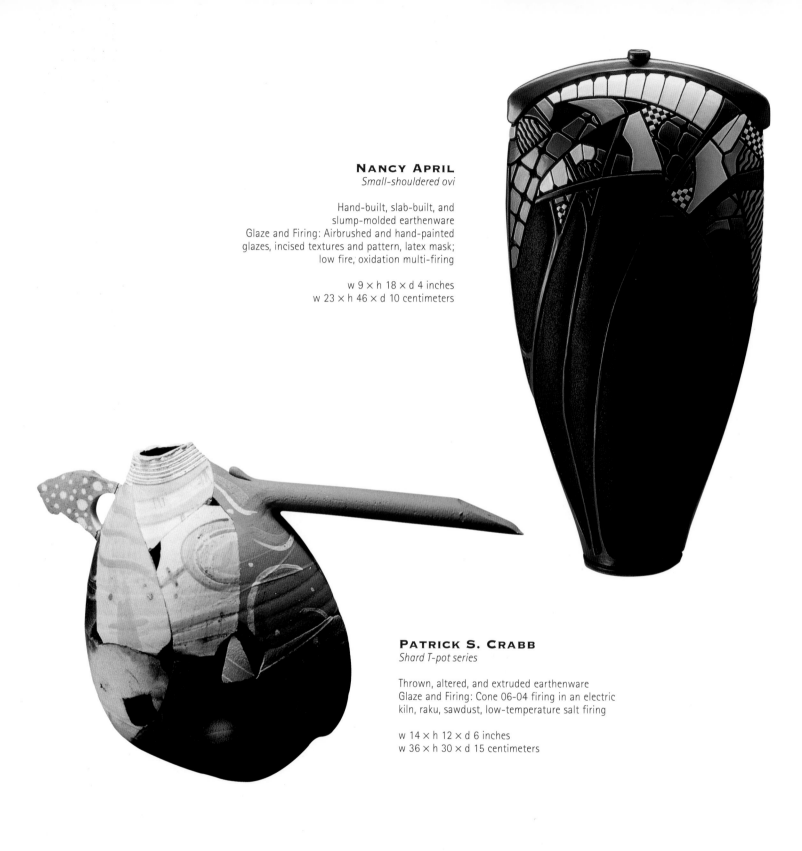

NANCY APRIL
Small-shouldered ovi

Hand-built, slab-built, and
slump-molded earthenware
Glaze and Firing: Airbrushed and hand-painted
glazes, incised textures and pattern, latex mask;
low fire, oxidation multi-firing

w 9 × h 18 × d 4 inches
w 23 × h 46 × d 10 centimeters

PATRICK S. CRABB
Shard T-pot series

Thrown, altered, and extruded earthenware
Glaze and Firing: Cone 06-04 firing in an electric
kiln, raku, sawdust, low-temperature salt firing

w 14 × h 12 × d 6 inches
w 36 × h 30 × d 15 centimeters

KATE WINN
Basket

Thrown and altered earthenware
Glaze and Firing: Majolica glazes, firing
in an electric kiln

w 14 × h 12 inches
w 36 × h 30 centimeters

SANDRA LUEHRSEN
Persian heart

Hand-built, coiled, and carved earthenware
Glaze and Firing: Layered slips and glazes, cone
06 oxidation firing in an electric kiln

w 14 × h 21 × d 13 inches
w 36 × h 53 × d 33 centimeters

BILL STEWART
T-pot

Hand-built earthenware
Glaze and Firing: Glazes, cone
06-04 oxidation multi-firing

w 5 × h 18 × d 8 inches
w 13 × h 46 × d 20 centimeters

JANE DILLON
Three cookie jars

Thrown, altered, and stacked earthenware
Glaze and Firing: Terra sigillata, slip, and glazes,
cone 04 oxidation firing

w 24 × h 10 × d 10 inches
w 61 × h 25 × d 25 centimeters

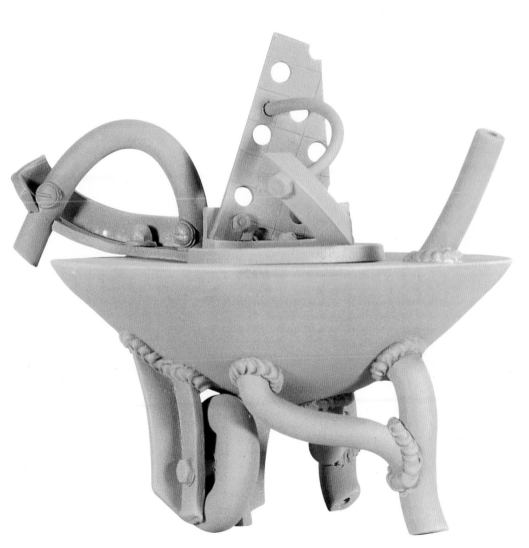

JAKE JACOBSON
#9603

Thrown, hand-built, extruded, and
press-molded earthenware
Glaze and Firing: Lithium, iron sulfate,
and oxidation firing

w 10 × h 7.5 × d 7.5 inches
w 25 × h 19 × d 19 centimeters

71

GRACE PILATO, IAN STAINTON
Untitled

Thrown and hand-carved raku
Glaze and Firing: Terra sigillata, burnished,
raku firing

w 13 × h 6 × d 13 inches
w 33 × h 15 × d 33 centimeters

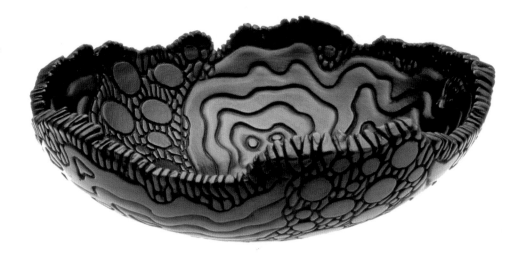

LORI MILLS
Tulip Barge

Thrown and altered earthenware
Glaze and Firing: Glazes, color slips, sgraffito,
slip-trailing, cone 05 and 04 oxidation firing in
an electric kiln

w 28 × h 18.5 × d 7.5 inches
w 71 × h 47 × d 19 centimeters

FRANK OZEREKO
Verdant

Hand-built earthenware
Glaze and Firing: Sprayed and painted glazes,
cone 04 firing in an electric kiln

w 22 × h 6 × d 3 inches
w 56 × h 15 × d 8 centimeters

CLAUDIA REESE
Carnival

Press-molded earthenware
Glaze and Firing: Clear glaze, sgraffito, cone 04

w 20 × h 20 × d 2.5 inches
w 51 × h 51 × d 6 centimeters

LINDA GANSTROM
Great Mother mugs

Slab-built earthenware
Glaze and Firing: Terra sigillata, cone 04
oxidation firing in an electric kiln

w 20 × h 6 × d 3 inches
w 51 × h 15 × d 8 centimeters

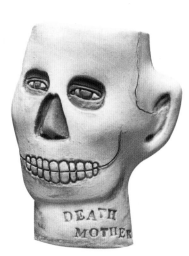

DON JONES
Cone with Dull Moon and Clouds

Thrown closed-cone earthenware
Glaze and Firing: Clear glaze, underglazes,
firing to cone 05

w 8 × h 18.5 × d 8 inches
w 20 × h 47 × d 20 centimeters

DAVID STABLEY
Vessel with open door

Thrown and slab-built earthenware
Glaze and Firing: Glazed interior, underglaze,
oxidation firing

w 18 × h 20 × d 12 inches
w 46 × h 51 × d 30 centimeters

LUCY BRESLIN
Summer Song #6

Thrown, altered, and hand-built earthenware
Glaze and Firing: Cone 04 firing in an
electric kiln

w 10 × h 9 × d 10 inches
w 25 × h 23 × d 25 centimeters

PETER SHIRE
Mayan Tableaux

Hand-built, slab-built, molded, and extruded
earthenware
Glaze and Firing: Clear underglaze, cone 06
firing

w 36 × h 21 × d 11 inches
w 93 × h 53 × d 28 centimeters

photo: William Nettles

SHELLIE Z. BROOKS
Crater Lake: Floating Basket
(collection of Edythe Zimmerman)

Press-molded and defloculated slip slabs poured
on plaster-slab earthenware
Glaze and Firing: Airbrushed underglaze, low-fire
firing in an electric kiln

w 12 × h 10 × d 12 inches
w 30 × h 25 × d 30 centimeters

BRADLEY KEYS
Buffalo Jump Pot

Thrown and assembled earthenware with
hand-built additions
Glaze and Firing: Terra sigillata, cone 04
firing in an electric kiln

h 20 × d 10 inches
h 51 × d 25 centimeters

POSEY BACOPOULOS
Beaked pitcher

Thrown, altered, and assembled
earthenware
Glaze and Firing: Majolica glaze, stains,
cone 04 firing in an electric kiln

w 7.5 × h 7 × d 3 inches
w 19 × h 18 × d 8 centimeters

RICHARD MILETTE
Staminos

Thrown and hand-built earthenware
Glaze and Firing: Glazes, China paints, decals,
luster, firing in an electric kiln

w 13.25 × h 11.25 × d 7 inches
w 34 × h 29 × d 18 centimeters

LESLIE ECKMANN
Red Hot

Thrown earthenware
Glaze and Firing: Clear glaze, oxidation firing

d 19 inches
d 48 centimeters

KEVIN A. MYERS
Untitled 11/1997

Thrown, altered, cut, incised, and
slip-trailed earthenware
Glaze and Firing: Chrome red glaze, cone 06
firing, cone 018 firing

w 6 × h 8 × d 8 inches
w 15 × h 20 × d 20 centimeters

DONNA GREEN
Vessel 1997

Coil-built earthenware
Glaze and Firing: Slips and oxidation under a
clear glaze, oxidation firing

w 18 × h 29.5 inches
w 46 × h 75 centimeters

KATHY ERTEMAN
Tall vessel

Slip-cast earthenware (from thrown original)
Glaze and Firing: Brushed clear glaze over black
carved underglaze, oxidation firing

w 8 × h 12 × d 8 inches
w 20 × h 30 × d 20 centimeters

photo: D. James Dee

DAVID CALVIN HEAPS
Left-handed winged cup with lap plate

Slip-cast earthenware
Glaze and Firing: Matte glaze, gloss green glaze,
oxidation firing

w 5.5 × h 4.5 × d 4 inches (cup)
w 14 × h 11 × d 10 centimeters (cup)
w 14 × h 2 × d 11.5 inches (plate)
w 36 × h 5 × d 39 centimeters (plate)

JARED JAFFE
Funky Teapot

Slip-cast and hand-built earthenware
Glaze and Firing: Low-fire firing in an
electric kiln

w 4 × h 9 × d 4 inches
w 10 × h 23 × d 10 centimeters

SYBILLE ZELDIN
Floral bowl

Hand-built earthenware
Glaze and Firing: Majolica glaze, low-fire
firing in an electric kiln

h 9 × d 16 inches
h 23 × d 41 centimeters

MARY CARROLL
Comparettia Speciosa

Hand-built earthenware with press-molded relief
Glaze and Firing: Polychrome glazes, cone 02
oxidation firing

w 16 × h 20 × d 16 inches
w 41 × h 51 × d 41 centimeters

SANDI PIERANTOZZI
Chimney-cap cruet set

Slab-built earthenware
Glaze and Firing: Low fire glaze, cone
04 bisque/cone 05 glaze, firing in an
electric kiln

w 10 × h 6 × d 5 inches
w 25 × h 15 × d 13 centimeters

ANNE SCHIESEL-HARRIS
Tumbling Teacups

Hand-built and slab-built
Glaze and Firing: Stains, glazes, cone 06
oxidation firing

w 13 × h 29 × d 4 inches
w 33 × h 74 × d 10 centimeters

MARK DERBY
French curve

Slab-built, press-molded, and
extruded earthenware
Glaze and Firing: Sprayed slip and glaze, soda
glaze over crackle slip during
oxidation firing

w 17 × h 8 × d 6 inches
w 43 × h 20 × d 15 centimeters

JOHN GOODHEART
Fra Bernardo's Sin Maker

Slab-built earthenware
Glaze and Firing: Dipped lithium glaze, cone 06
oxidation firing in an electric kiln

w 9 × h 7 × d 3 inches
w 23 × h 18 × d 8 centimeters

DONNA MCGEE
Elizabeth Man

Thrown and altered earthenware with
coil handles
Glaze and Firing: Sgraffito, slips,
underglazes, cone 03 oxidation firing

w 9 × h 14 × d 7 inches
w 23 × h 36 × d 18 centimeters

JAMES C. WATKINS
Raku teapot

Thrown and hand-built earthenware
Glaze and Firing: Unglazed, terra sigillata, raku
glaze, sagger firing

w 14 × h 15 inches
w 36 × h 38 centimeters

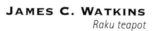

PIERO FENCI
Sakai Shaker Hatbox

Hand-built earthenware
Glaze and Firing: Cone 06-04 raku firing

w 15 × h 9 × d 15 inches
w 38 × h 23 × d 38 centimeters

JENNIE BIRELINE
Amazon Origami #3

Hand-built and slab-built earthenware
Glaze and Firing: Terra sigillata, firing to cone 04

h 21.75 inches
h 56 centimeters

ELAINE ALT
Waves

Thrown and hand-built earthenware
Glaze and Firing: Underglazes and luster,
multi-firing in an electric kiln

w 6.5 × h 15 inches
w 17 × h 38 centimeters

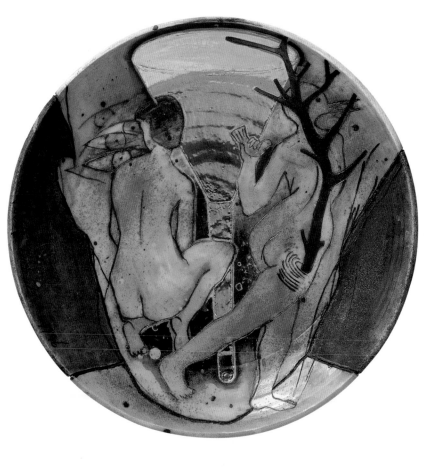

STAN WELSH, MARGITTA DIETRICK
Golden Funnel—1997

Thrown earthenware
Glaze and Firing: Cone 04 underglazes, cone 04 glazes, cone 018 gold luster, oxidation firing

w 24 × h 24 × d 4 inches
w 61 × h 61 × d 10 centimeters

CLARK BURGAN
Dinner set

Thrown earthenware
Glaze and Firing: Cone 04 firing in an electric kiln

w 14 × h 3 inches (largest plate)
w 36 × h 8 centimeters (largest plate)

WOODY HUGHES
Steam-iron teapot

Thrown, altered, and assembled
earthenware
Glaze and Firing: Terra sigillata, transparent
glazes, firing in an electric kiln

w 14 × h 9 × d 4 inches
w 36 × h 23 × d 10 centimeters

DIANE KENNEY
Bird Platter

Thrown earthenware
Glaze and Firing: Majolica glaze,
cone 05 firing in an electric kiln

w 20 × h 3 × d 2.5 inches
w 51 × h 8 × d 6 centimeters

RICHARD HIRSCH
Primal Cup #2

Thrown and hand-built earthenware
Glaze and Firing: Low-fire firing in an
electric kiln, raku

w 10 × h 8.75 × d 5 inches
w 25 × h 22.5 × d 13 centimeters

SUSAN BOSTWICK
The Harvest of Burden and Delight

Hand-built earthenware
Glaze and Firing: Layered underglazes and
glazes, oxidation firing in an electric kiln

w 5 × h 7 × d 4 inches
w 13 × h 18 × d 10 centimeters

JUDY KOGOD COLWELL
Melon vase

Hand-built earthenware
Glaze and Firing: Clear glaze, underglaze slips,
stains, slip trailing, resists, cone 05 firing in an
electric kiln

w 6 × h 16 × d 2 inches
w 15 × h 41 × d 5 centimeters

ROBERT BEDE CLARKE
Small Nest of the Body #1

Thrown earthenware with altered rim
Glaze and Firing: Colored engobes, stain, frit
wash, oxidation firing in an electric kiln

w 28 × h 28 × d 5 inches
w 71 × h 71 × d 13 centimeters

GREG PAYCE
Wake

Thrown earthenware using templates
Glaze and Firing: Terra sigillata exterior, glazed
interior, cone 04 oxidation firing

w 21.5 × h 8.5 × d 7 inches
w 55 × h 21 × d 18 centimeters

WESLEY ANDEREGG
Goblets

Pinched earthenware
Glaze and Firing: Low-fire glazes
and slips, firing in an electric kiln

w 3 × h 7 × d 2 inches
w 8 × h 18 × d 5 centimeters

ROSALIE WYNKOOP
Rubaiyat teapot

Thrown and hand-built earthenware
Glaze and Firing: Majolica glaze, gold luster,
China paint; cone 05 and cone 018 firing
in an electric kiln

w 4.5 × h 12 × d 9 inches
w 11 × h 30 × d 23 centimeters

CLAUDETTE GERHOLD, PAUL GERHOLD
Thrown raku body

Glaze and Firing: Brushed silver and tin, raku firing in electric kiln

w 8 × h 18 × d 8 inches
w 20 × h 46 × d 20 centimeters

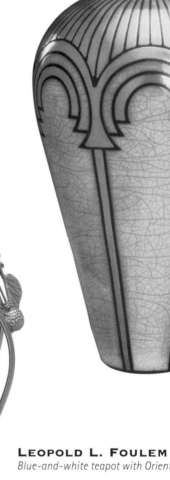

LEOPOLD L. FOULEM
Blue-and-white teapot with Oriental Landscapes

Hand-built earthenware
Glaze and Firing: Decals, firing in an electric kiln

w 11.75 × h 11.75 × d 5.5 inches
w 30 × h 30 × d 14 centimeters

ROBERT BEDE CLARKE
Minoan (#3)

Thrown earthenware
Glaze and Firing: Engobes and stains,
sagger firing

w 16 × h 20 × d 16 inches
w 41 × h 51 × d 41 centimeters

STEVE DAVIS-ROSENBAUM
Creamer

Thrown earthenware
Glaze and Firing: Majolica glaze, colored
stains, firing in an electric kiln

w 3.5 × h 5 inches
w 9 × h 13 centimeters

GEORGE McCAULEY
Light Headed Goddess of The Snake Tower

Thrown and slab-built earthenware
Glaze and Firing: Terra sigillata, glaze,
soda firing to cone 01

w 9.25 × h 22.5 inches
w 24 × h 57 centimeters

JEROD MORRIS
Creamer

Press-molded and slab-built earthenware
Glaze and Firing: Low-fire lithium glazes,
multi-firing in electric kiln

w 5 × h 7 × d 3 inches
w 13 × h 18 × d 8 centimeters

EMMETT LEADER
Animal in Wagon #2

Thrown and hand-built earthenware
Glaze and Firing: Terra sigillata,
firing in an electric kiln

w 8 × h 15 × d 6 inches
w 20 × h 38 × d 15 centimeters

Porcelain is a fine-grained clay made up of kaolin with a high quartz and feldspar content. Porcelain is fired at high temperatures. White ware pottery is named for its white or cream-colored body.

Porc

elain & White Ware

Michael Lambert .... *Java Jig*
.... coffee and tea set

Cast and assembled porcelain

Glaze and Firing: Black mat
glaze, oxidation firing
coffee pot: w 9 x h 10 x d 4 inches
w 23 x h 25 x d 10 centimeters

Deanna J. Eckels .... *Fish bowl*

Thrown and texturized porcelain

Glaze and Firing: Mason stain washes,
brushed underglazes, and clear glaze with
sgraffito, cone 10 reduction firing
h 5 x d 18 inches
h 13 x d 46 centimeters

Les Lawrence .... *New Vision Teapot #0727950*

Slab-built porcelain

Glaze and Firing: Unglazed, cone·10
oxidation firing in an electric kiln
w 14 x h 8 x d 2.5 inches
w 35 x h 21 x d 6 centimeters

Kathryn E. Narrow .... *Peach Pot #35*

Thrown and carved porcelain

Glaze and Firing: Copper, satin, and mat
glazes with ink, cone 6 gas reduction firing
w 8 x h 7.5 inches
w 20 x h 9 centimeters

Andy Brayman .... Teapot

Thrown porcelain

Glaze and Firing: Kaolin flashing slip,
wood-firing
w 8 x h 10 x d 6 inches
w 20 x h 25 x d 15 centimeters

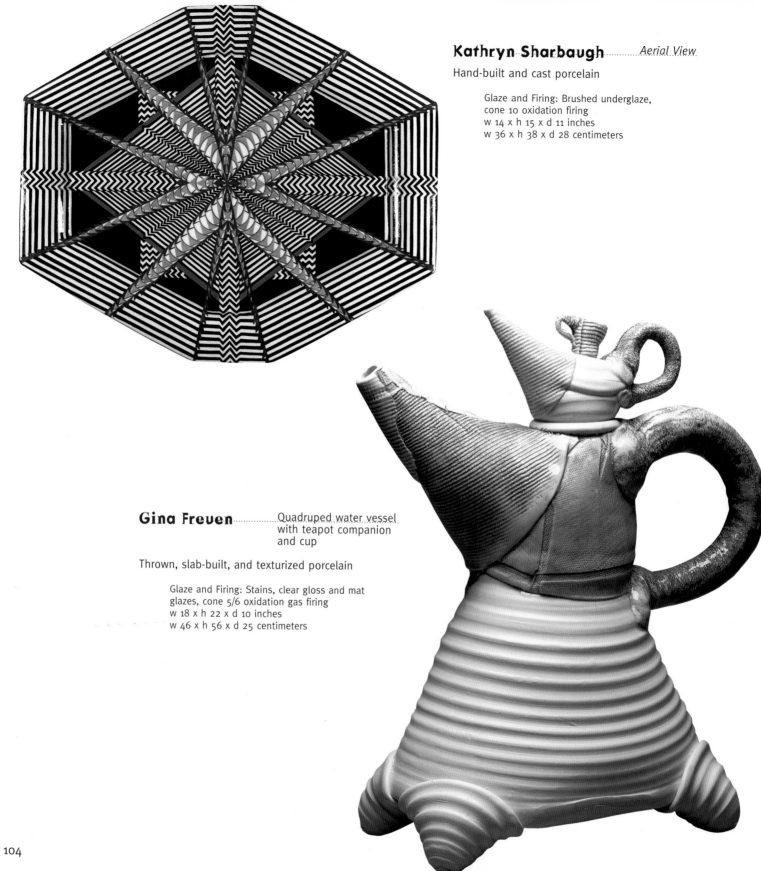

Kathryn Sharbaugh ....*Aerial View*

Hand-built and cast porcelain

Glaze and Firing: Brushed underglaze,
cone 10 oxidation firing
w 14 x h 15 x d 11 inches
w 36 x h 38 x d 28 centimeters

Gina Freuen ....Quadruped water vessel
with teapot companion
and cup

Thrown, slab-built, and texturized porcelain

Glaze and Firing: Stains, clear gloss and mat
glazes, cone 5/6 oxidation gas firing
w 18 x h 22 x d 10 inches
w 46 x h 56 x d 25 centimeters

104

Peg Malloy .... Pitcher

Thrown porcelain

Glaze and Firing: Shino slip,
wood-firing in bourry-box kiln
w 7 x h 9 x d 5.5 inches
w 18 x h 23 x d 14 centimeters

Gwen Heffner .... Double cut bowl

Thrown and altered porcelain

Glaze and Firing: Unglazed, cone 9 oxidation firing
w 10 x h 11 inches
w 25 x h 28 centimeters

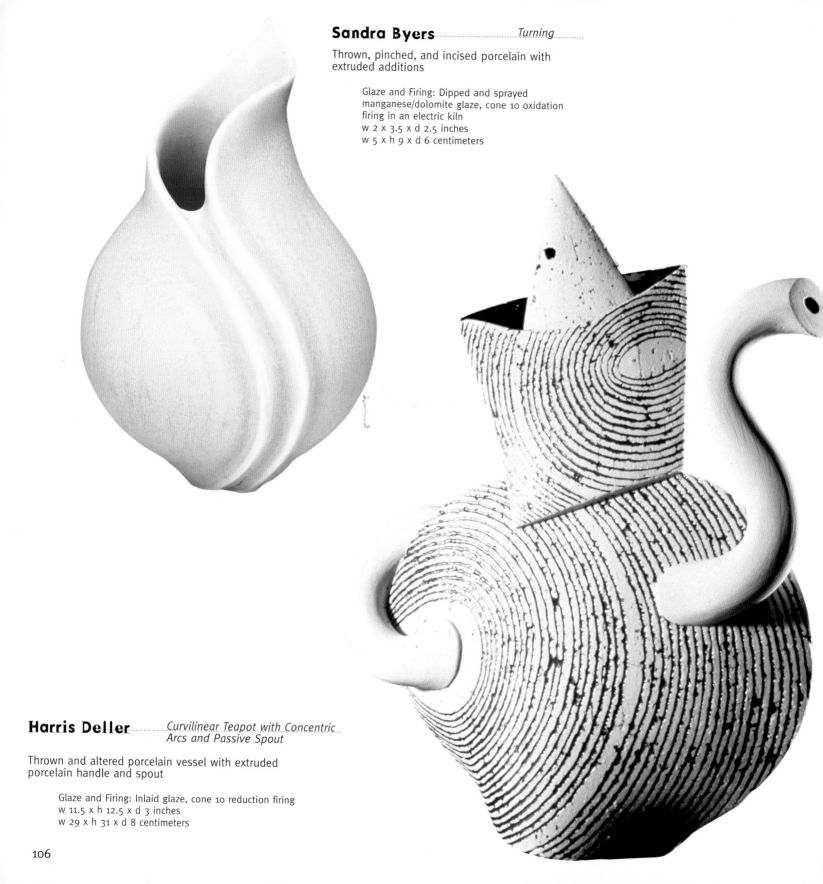

Sandra Byers .... *Turning*

Thrown, pinched, and incised porcelain with
extruded additions

    Glaze and Firing: Dipped and sprayed
    manganese/dolomite glaze, cone 10 oxidation
    firing in an electric kiln
    w 2 x 3.5 x d 2.5 inches
    w 5 x h 9 x d 6 centimeters

Harris Deller .... *Curvilinear Teapot with Concentric*
                                        Arcs and Passive Spout

Thrown and altered porcelain vessel with extruded
porcelain handle and spout

    Glaze and Firing: Inlaid glaze, cone 10 reduction firing
    w 11.5 x h 12.5 x d 3 inches
    w 29 x h 31 x d 8 centimeters

Charles B. Nalle
Spiral lid teapot

Cast white ware

Glaze and Firing: Glaze over glaze, cone 6
oxidation firing
w 10 x h 10 x d 6 inches
w 25 x h 25 x d 15 centimeters

Elizabeth Roman
Vessel #1

Thrown and altered porcelain

Glaze and Firing: Airbrushed Albany slip-glaze,
cone 10 gas firing
h 11 x d 22 inches
h 28 x d 56 centimeters

Elizabeth A. Plepis
Rock-a-Bye teapot

Slipcast mold (made from vegetable and fruit forms)
with low-fire talc

Glaze and Firing: Yellow and blue slip-glazes, sagger
firing with pine needles and pine cones for terra cotta
color
w 6 x h 8 inches
w 15 x h 20 centimeters

Denise Woodward .... Gravy boat ......

Thrown and altered porcelain

> Glaze and Firing: Green and blue glass glaze,
> high-fire reduction firing
> w 9 x h 7 x d 5 inches
> w 23 x h 18 x d 13 centimeters

Joanne Kirkland .... Vessel

Thrown porcelain

> Glaze and Firing: Multi-layered glaze with w
> resist and sgraffito, cone 10/11 firing
> w 7 x h 7.5 inches
> w 18 x h 19 centimeters

Lynn Goodman .... Vase ....

Thrown, carved, and trimmed porcelain

> Glaze and Firing: Multi-glaze, stains, and gold
> luster, oxidation firing in an electric kiln
> w 6 x h 11 inches
> w 15 x h 28 centimeters

Shirley Johnson············Dessert plates

Thrown porcelain

> Glaze and Firing: Poured glaze and slip-trailed,
> gas reduction firing
> w 8 x h 1.5 inches
> w 20 x h 4 centimeters

Dale Huffman············Pitcher

Thrown porcelain

> Glaze and Firing: Cone 8 reduction firing
> w 6.5 x h 6.5 x d 5 inches
> w 17 x h 17 x d 13 centimeters

Shirley Johnson············Bowls

Thrown porcelain

> Glaze and Firing: Glazes, cone 10 gas reduction
> firing
> w 6 x h 3 inches
> w 15 x h 8 centimeters

Robert Levine .... *Low vessel*

Thrown porcelain

> Glaze and Firing: Crystalline glaze, dripped copper
> glaze, overglaze, high-fire and low-fire multi-firing
> in an electric kiln
> h 6 x d 22 inches
> h 15 x d 56 centimeters

Sally Bowen Prange .... *Wrecked Vessel
with Celebration Glaze*

Thrown, altered, and hand-built porcelain

> Glaze and Firing: Gloss glaze, copper-reduction
> red glaze, and luster, cone 9 reduction firing
> w 7 x h 12 x d 7.5 inches
> w 18 x h 31 x d 19 centimeters

Alan and Brenda Newman .... Flared goblets

Slip cast and epoxied porcelain

Glaze and Firing: Nickel-chrome stain over
titanium mat glaze, cone 6 firing in an electric kiln
w 3.5 x h 9 inches
w 8 x h 22 centimeters

Colby Parsons-O'Keefe .... *Precarious Bird*

Hand-built porcelain

Glaze and Firing: Burnished black slip,
cone 10 oxidation firing in an electric kiln
w 9 x h 16 inches
w 23 x h 41 centimeters

ichael Wainwright .... Bowls

b-built porcelain

Glaze and Firing: Mat white glaze, 22-karat gold and
platinum lusters, cone 6 firing in an electric kiln
Large bowl w 13 x h 4 inches
Large bowl w 33 x h 10 centimeters
Medium bowl w 9.5 x h 3.5 inches
Medium bowl w 24 x h 9 centimeters
Small bowl w 5.5 x h 2 inches
Small bowl w 14 x h 5 centimeters

111

Geoffrey Wheeler Compote

Thrown, altered, and assembled porcelain

Glaze and Firing: Copper celadon glaze, cone
10 soda firing
w 14 x h 12 x d 8 inches
w 36 x h 31 x d 20 centimeters

Barbara L. Frey *Settle Down Teapot #1*

Hand-built porcelain

Glaze and Firing: Glazed interior, slip-glazed exterior
with sgraffito, cone 6 oxidation firing
w 8 x h 7 x d 4 inches
w 20 x h 17 x d 10 centimeters

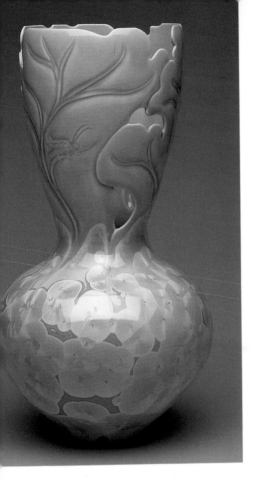

Ronalee Herrmann and Alfred Stolken .... Vessel

Thrown, carved, and reticulated porcelain

Glaze and Firing: Crystalline glaze, cone 12
oxidation firing
w 5 x h 9 inches
w 13 x h 23 centimeters

Geoffrey Wheeler .... Vase

Thrown porcelain

Glaze and Firing: Celadon glaze, cone 10 gas
reduction firing
w 8.5 x h 14 x d 8.5 inches
w 22 x h 36 x d 22 centimeters

113

Gertrude Graham Smith Teapot

Thrown and faceted porcelain

Glaze and Firing: Slip glaze, soda firing
w 6 x h 5.5 x d 9 inches
w 15 x h 13 x d 23 centimeters

Henri Martin Bowl

Thrown porcelain

Glaze and Firing: Poured copper-red glaze,
cone 9 reduction firing
w 13 x h 5.5 inches
w 32.5 x h 14 centimeters

John Tilton Vase

Thrown porcelain

Glaze and Firing: Dipped and sprayed
mat crystalline glazes, cone 10 reduction
multi-firing
w 5 x h 10 x d 5 inches
w 13 x h 26 x d 13 centimeters

Carol Sevick......................*Coral Pool*........

Hand-built porcelain

> Glaze and Firing: Sprayed glaze, cone 10
> oxidation firing in an electric kiln
> w 14 x h 6 x d 14 inches
> w 36 x h 15 x d 36 centimeters

Don R. Davis......................Round bowl

Thrown porcelain

> Glaze and Firing: Clear glaze interior, cobalt-blue
> slip-trailed and black oxide glaze exterior, cone 7
> reduction firing
> w 11 x h 6.5 x d 11 inches
> w 28 x h 16 x d 28 centimeters

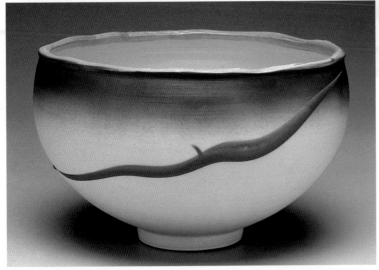

Chris Staley......................*Vessel on tray*..............

Thrown and altered porcelain vessel, hand-built
black stoneware tray

> Glaze and Firing: High-fire reduction firing
> w 10 x h 8 x d 15 inches
> w 25 x h 20 x d 38 centimeters

115

Anne Schiesel-Harris Symmetrical vessel

Slab-built, hand-built, and imprinted porcelain

Glaze and Firing: Stains and glazes, cone 6 oxidation firing
w 12 x h 23 x d 7 inches
w 31 x h 58 x d 18 centimeters

Berry Matthews Red and green teapot

Hand-built, cast, and slab-built porcelain

Glaze and Firing: Copper glaze,
cone 10 reduction firing
w 3 x h 6.5 x d 7.5 inches
w 8 x h 16 x d 19 centimeters

Marianne Weinberg-Benson *A Bishop "My Vision Is Right"*

Thrown porcelain

Glaze and Firing: High-fire gloss glazes, sprayed acrylic, and drawings with powdered pastels, gas oxidation firing
w 8 x h 24 x d 8 inches
w 20 x h 61 x d 20 centimeters

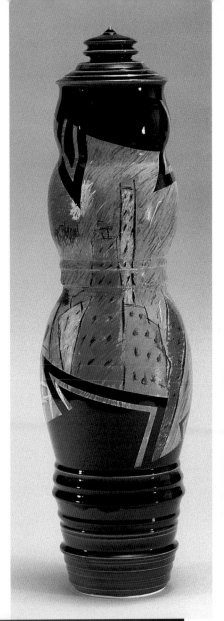

ephen Fabrico *Low teapot*

st and assembled porcelain

Glaze and Firing: Expansion glaze, cone 10 gas firing
w 9 x h 13 x d 13 inches
w 23 x h 33 x d 33 centimeters

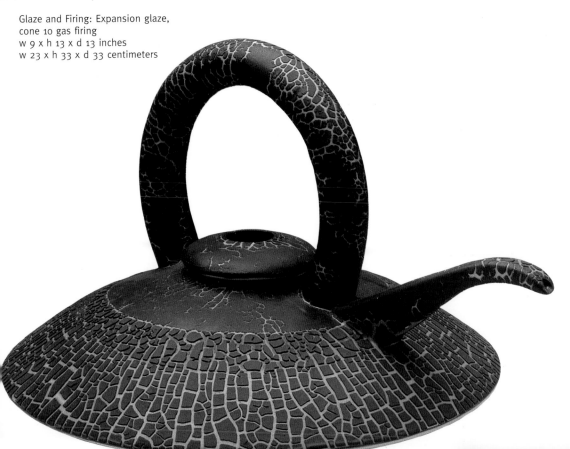

Maren Kloppmann *Vessel*

Hand-built and coil-built porcelain

Glaze and Firing: Terra sigillata, cone 10 soda firing
w 32 x h 8 x d 15 inches
w 81 x h 20 x d 38 centimeters

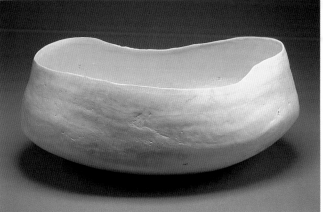

117

Earline Allen .... *Midsummer's Dream* ......
vessel

Thrown and hand-built porcelain

> Glaze and Firing: Glaze interior, slip exterior,
> cone 6 oxidation firing
> w 7 x h 20 inches
> w 18 x h 51 centimeters

Berry Matthews ..... Black striped teapot ......

Hand-built and slab-built porcelain

> Glaze and Firing: Black slip with clear glaze,
> cone 10 oxidation firing
> w 10 x h 5 x d 9 inches
> w 25 x h 13 x d 23 centimeters

Hideaki Miyamura *Yohen-Temmoku* vase

Thrown porcelain

Glaze and Firing: Yohen-temmoku glaze, cone 10 oxidation firing
w 7.5 x h 13.5 x d 7.5 inches
w 18 x h 34 x d 18 centimeters

D. Langford Kühn *Exotica*

Thrown and hammered porcelain

Glaze and Firing: Underglazes, lusters, enamel overglazes, cone 10 multi-firing
w 9 x h 10 x d 9 inches
w 23 x h 25 x d 23 centimeters

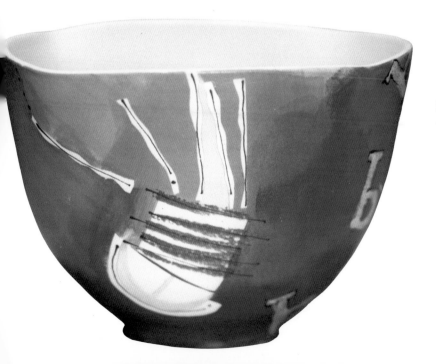

Shawn Lyn Panepinto *Bowl*

Thrown and altered porcelain

Glaze and Firing: Brushed underglaze, satin clear glaze exterior, cone 6 firing in an electric kiln
w 7.5 x h 5.5 inches
w 18 x h 13 centimeters

Laura Barov .... Vessel ....

Hand-built, coiled, and pinched porcelain

Glaze and Firing: Terra sigillata,
cone 10 reduction firing
w 7 x h 14 inches
w 18 x h 36 centimeters

Jay Lacouture .... Teapot ......

Thrown and assembled porcelain

Glaze and Firing: Slips and soda vapor glazes,
cone 8 firing
w 9.5 x h 12 x d 6 inches
w 24 x h 31 x d 15 centimeters

Stephen Fabrico   Teapots

Cast, assembled, and sandblasted porcelain

> Glaze and Firing: Black gloss and black mat
> glazes over copper surface, cone 10 gas firing
> w 10 x h 12 x d 8 inches
> w 25 x h 31 x d 20 centimeters

Janel Jacobson   *Autumn Aria*

Thrown and hand-carved porcelain

> Glaze and Firing: Celadon glaze, cone 10 gas
> reduction firing
> w 2.5 x h 1 inches
> w 6 x h 3 centimeters

Kate Inskeep .... *Oak* vessel

Hand-built porcelain

Glaze and Firing: Black slip and soda-ash glazes with stencils, multi-firing with gas soda and in an electric kiln
w 16 x h 17 x d 4 inches
w 41 x h 43 x d 10 centimeters

Wendy Dubin .... Soy bottle

Thrown and altered porcelain

Glaze and Firing: Glaze, oxidation firing
w 4.5 x h 5.5 x d 3
w 12 x h 14 x d 8 centimeters

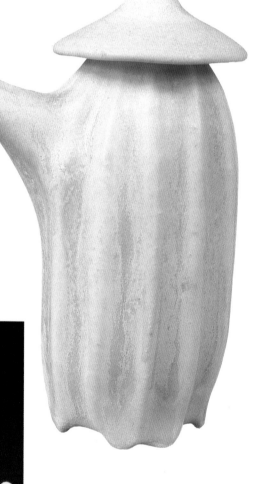

Malcolm Davis .... Shino tea bowl

Thrown porcelain

Glaze and Firing: Red shino carbon-trap glaze, cone 10 reduction firing
w 3 x h 3.5 x d 3 inches
w 8 x h 9 x d 8 centimeters

Marsha Silverman .... Teapot

Thrown and altered porcelain

Glaze and Firing: Colored glaze, cone 9 firing in an electric kiln
w 6.5 x h 8 inches
w 17 x h 20 centimeters

Vincent Suez — *Heron's Nest*

Thrown and incised porcelain

Glaze and Firing: Copper glaze,
cone 6 oxidation firing
w 11 x h 17 x d 10 inches
w 28 x h 43 x d 25 centimeters

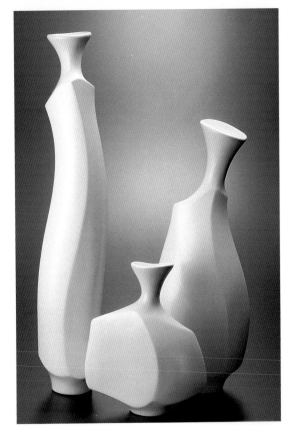

Scott Tubby — *Three Faceted Forms*

Cast low-fire porcelain

Glaze and Firing: Unglazed and polished,
cone 010 firing
w 3.5 x h 18 x d 3 inches
w 9 x h 46 x d 8 centimeters

Eve Fleck — Baking dish/bowl

Thrown porcelain

Glaze and Firing: Brushed underglaze, stains, and
dipped clear glaze, cone 7 oxidation firing
h 5 x d 12 inches
h 13 x d 31 centimeters

123

Jerry Rothman .... *Ritual vessel*

Thrown and hand-built vitreous china

Glaze and Firing: Glaze, firing in gas kiln
w 12 x h 16 x d 8 inches
w 31 x h 41 x d 20 centimeters

Marian Haigh .... *Small Antler bowl*

Hand-built with extruded coils and thin slabs,
press molds of antlers, low-fire white ware

Glaze and Firing: Low-fire mat glaze, cone 04 firing, smoked with minimal sawdust in a metal
sagger in an electric kiln
w 13 x h 4 x d 13 inches
w 33 x h 10 x d 33 centimeters

Linda Arndt............*Polkadot Bottles I & II*............

Hand-built, with mold extruded low-fire white ware

Glaze and Firing: Underglaze, engobes, clear glaze, and
sgraffito, cone 04, cone 05, cone 022 multi-firing
Bottle I w 4 x h 16 x d 4 inches
Bottle I w 10 x h 40 x d 10 centimeters
Bottle II w 4 x h 14 x d 4 inches
Bottle II w 10 x h 36 x d 10 centimeters

Lynn Smiser Bowers............*Fishbone* platter......

Hand-built and slab-built high-fire porcelain

Glaze and Firing: Reduction glazes with wax resists,
stencils, and sponging, cone 10 gas reduction
firing in a soft-brick kiln
w 18 x h 14 x d 2 inches
w 48 x h 38 x d 5 centimeters

Rebecca Harvey .... *Teapot Variation*

Thrown and press-molded porcelain

Glaze and Firing: Polychrome glazes, oxidation firing
w 6 x h 8 x d 9 inches
w 15 x h 20 x d 23 centimeters

Wayne Bates .... *Large Platter #4*

Thrown porcelain

Glaze and Firing: Engobes and glazes with sgraffito,
cone 6 gas firing in a fiber kiln
h 1.5 x d 16 inches
h 4 x d 41 centimeters

Elsa Rady ..... Still Life #57 ....

Thrown, trimmed, carved, sculpted,
and epoxied porcelain

Glaze and Firing: Sprayed glaze, cone 7
oxidation firing
w 14.5 x h 19.5 x d 14.5 inches
w 36 x h 50 x d 37 centimeters

Sunkong Chung ..... Eggbowls ....

Cast colored porcelain

Glaze and Firing: Clear glaze, cone 8 firing in an
electric kiln
large eggbowl w 13 x h 8 x d 3 inches
large eggbowl w 33 x h 20 x d 8 centimeters
small eggbowl w 9 x h 6 x d 2 inches
small eggbowl w 23 x h 15 x d 5 centimeters

Elaine Woldorsky — *Birch Tree with Woodpecker*

Thrown porcelain

Glaze and Firing: Copper-red glaze with black decoration, cone 10 gas firing
w 3 x h 6.5 x d 3 inches
w 8 x h 17 x d 8 centimeters

Andrea M. Fábrega — *Miniature pottery*

Thrown and trimmed porcelain

Glaze and Firing: Reduction glazes with slips, high-fire reduction firing
h 1.5 x d 1 inches
h 5 x d 3 centimeters

Donna Anderegg — *Teapot with cups*

Thrown porcelain

Glaze and Firing: Slips, salt-firing
w 8 x h 8 x d 5 inches
w 20 x h 20 x d 13 centimeters

Regis C. Brodie — *Blue And Green Form*

Thrown, hand-built, and paddled porcelain

Glaze and Firing: Glaze and stain, cone 9/10 reduction firing
w 6 x h 23 inches
w 15 x h 58 centimeters

Ruth E. Allan · · · · · · · *Bound Earth* · · · · · · · · · · · · ·

Thrown porcelain

Glaze and Firing: Unglazed and polished,
salt reduction sagger-firing in a gas kiln
w 17 x h 9 x d 8 inches
w 43 x h 23 x d 20 centimeters

Karen Thuesen Massaro · · · · · · · *Straw Plums*

Assembled and cast porcelain

Glaze and Firing: Brushed underglaze, glaze, and china
paints, cone 10 oxidation firing in an electric kiln
w 9.5 x h 8.5 x d 5 inches
w 25 x h 22 x d 11 centimeters

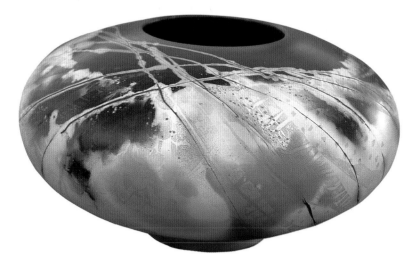

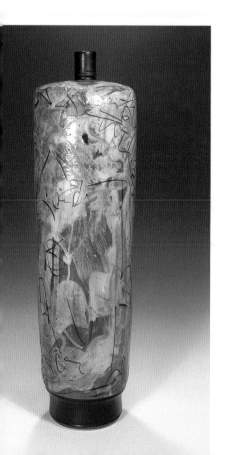

Susan Meredith Bunzl Teapot

Thrown and extruded porcelain

Glaze and Firing: White barium mat glaze, and
inlaid colored porcelain, cone 018 gas firing
h 9.5 x d 7 inches
h 24 x d 18 centimeters

Stephen Fabrico Triangle teapot and
miniature teapot

Cast, thrown, and assembled porcelain

Glaze and Firing: Dipped and sprayed glaze,
cone 9/10 gas firing
Triangle teapot w 12 x h 4 x d 13 inches
Triangle teapot w 31 x h 10 x d 33 centimeters
Miniature teapot w 3.5 x h 2.5 x d 4 inches
Miniature teapot w 9 x h 6 x d 10 centimeters

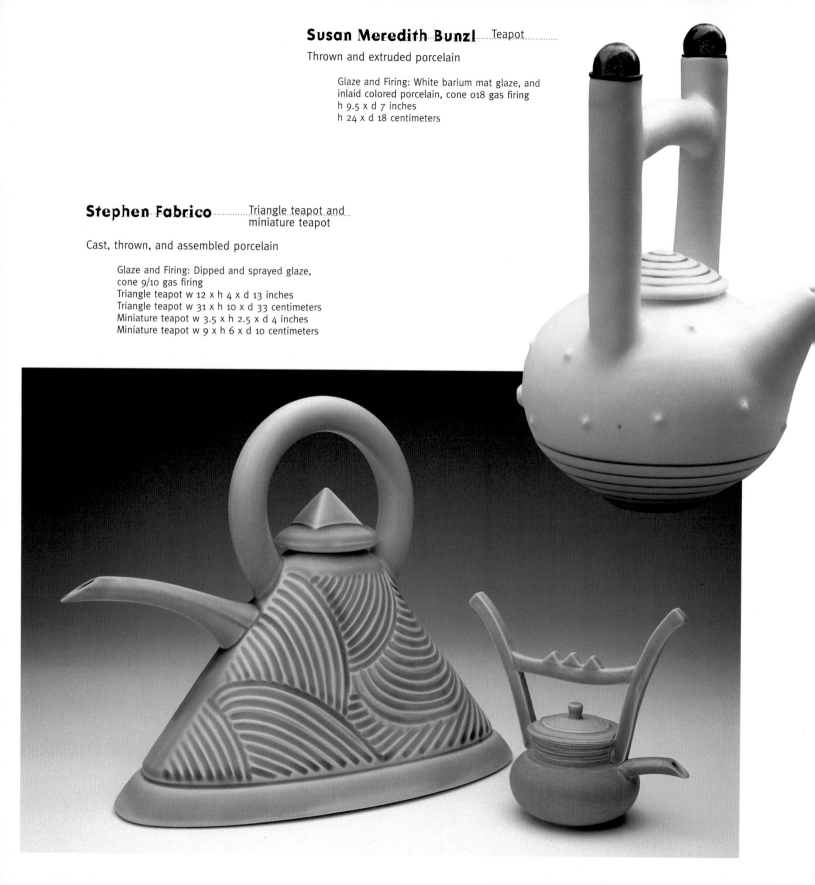

Paul Mathieu............*Still Life with Teapot*....

Thrown porcelain

Glaze and Firing: Clear glaze, stains,
overglazes, and lusters, cone 10 oxidation firing
w 13 x h 6 x d 13 inches
w 35 x h 15 x d 35 centimeters

Ian Jones............Faceted vase....

Wheel-thrown and cut porcelain and stoneware

Glaze and Firing: Raw glaze on inside, cone 13
firing in an anagama kiln
w 9.5 x h 19 inches
w 24 x h 48 centimeters

Jeroen Bechtold............*Eggshell vase*....

Cast, thrown, hand-built, and carved porcelain

Glaze and Firing: Multi-glazing, oxidation
multi-firing in gas kiln
w 9 x h 8 inches
w 22 x h 20 centimeters

Yuriko Matsuda
Basket with an Artichoke

Cast and slab-built porcelain

Glaze and Firing: High-fire clear glaze and enamel
overglaze, cone 9 reduction, cone 17 multi-firing
w 9 x h 13 x d 8 inches
w 22 x h 32 x d 19 centimeters

Sarah Jaeger
Teapot and two cups

Thrown porcelain with reed handle

Glaze and Firing: Multi-layered glazes with wax
resist, cone 10/11 reduction firing
Teapot w 8.5 x h 10 x d 7 inches
Teapot w 22 x h 25 x d 18 centimeters
Cups h 3 inches
Cups h 8 centimeters

Tim Strachan
The Essence

Thrown and hand-carved porcelain

Glaze and Firing: Lapidary polished,
cone 019 oxidation firing
w 8 x h 13 inches
w 19 x h 32 centimeters

Carolyn Chester ...... Bowl

Thrown porcelain

Glaze and Firing: Slip underglaze, cone 9
oxidation firing
w 6 x h 7 inches
w 15 x h 18 centimeters

Cliff Lee ...... Three imperial yellow vases

Thrown, altered, carved, and applied porcelain

Glaze and Firing: Monochrome glaze, high-fire reduction firing
#1 w 7 x h 12 inches
#1 w 18 x h 31 centimeters
#2 w 5 x h 9 inches
#2 w 13 x h 23 centimeters
#3 w 6.5 x h 10 inches
#3 w 17 x h 25 centimeters

Masako Miyata ...... *Furoshiki*

Hand-built white ware

Glaze and Firing: Underglaze and glaze, oxidation
firing
w 26 x h 8.5 x d 22 inches
w 66 x h 22 x d 56 centimeters

Elsa Rady........................*Still Life #52*

Thrown, trimmed, carved, sculpted, and epoxied porcelain

> Glaze and Firing: Sprayed glaze, cone 7 oxidation firing
> w 14 x h 24 x d 10 inches
> w 36 x h 61 x.d 25 centimeters

Mark Bell........................Bowl........................

Thrown porcelain

> Glaze and Firing: Sprayed reduction glaze, cone 10 reduction firing
> w 10 x h 3.5 x d 10 inches
> w 25 x h 9 x d 25 centimeters

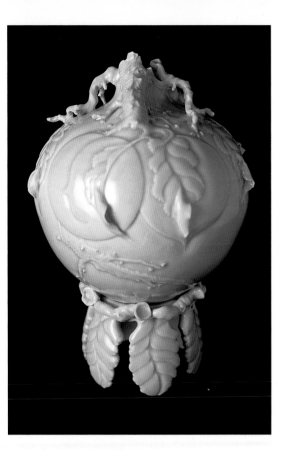

Carol Eder  *Fluid Clay V*

Thrown and altered porcelain

> Glaze and Firing: Brushed temmoku and
> shino glazes
> w 8 x h 4 x d 5 inches
> w 20 x h 10 x d 13 centimeters

Cliff Lee *Peach vase*

Thrown, altered, carved, and applied porcelain

> Glaze and Firing: Monochrome glaze, high-fire
> reduction firing
> w 7.5 x h 12.5 inches
> w 19 x h 32 centimeters

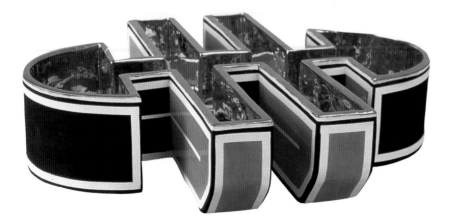

Roberta Griffith *Nikko Curvature* from *Nikko Transfer* series

Hand-built, low-fire white ware with hand-built, cut, and
assembled modules

> Glaze and Firing: clear glaze, gold luster overglaze interior,
> underglaze exterior, cone 04, cone 018 oxidation multi-firing
> in an electric kiln
> w 12.5 x h 4 x d 14.5 inches
> w 31 x h 10 x d 35 centimeters

SUNYONG CHUNG
Small bowls

Hump-molded porcelain
Glaze and Firing: Clear glaze, high-temperature
firing in an electric kiln

h 4.5 × d 6 inches
h 11 × d 15 centimeters

ELSA RADY
Still Life #70

Thrown and carved porcelain
Glaze and Firing: Spray, cone 8 firing

w 18 × h 18 × d 11 inches
w 46 × h 46 × d 28 centimeters

BARBARA SEBASTIAN
Spiral

Thrown porcelain
Glaze and Firing: Copper red glaze,
cone 10 firing

w 5 × h 2 × d 4 inches
w 13 × h 5 × d 10 centimeters

ELIZABETH ROMAN
Sapplio

Thrown and altered porcelain
Glaze and Firing: Airbrushed cushing semi-matte
glaze, cone 10 oxidation firing

w 6 × h 12.5 × d 6 inches
w 15 × h 32 × d 15 centimeters

JOANNE KIRKLAND
Cobalt jar

Thrown and altered porcelain
Glaze and Firing: Wax resist, multi-colored
layering, sgraffito, cone 10 and cone 11 firing
in a natural gas downdraft kiln

w 5 × h 3.75 inches
w 13 × h 10 centimeters

LES LAWRENCE
New Vision—Teapot #A60901

Hand-built porcelain
Glaze and Firing: Single firing

w 3 × h 9 × d 15 inches
w 8 × h 23 × d 38 centimeters

LAURA WILENSKY
Neighborly Advice

Hand-built porcelain
Glaze and Firing: Cone 10 clear with
underglaze stains, cone 018 china paints,
firing in an electric kiln

w 9 × h 6 × d 6 inches
w 23 × h 15 × d 15 centimeters

VICTORIA D. CHRISTEN
Three blue cups

Thrown and altered porcelain
Glaze and Firing: Copper glaze, cone 10 soda
firing, cone 10 oxidation firing

w 3 × h 3 × d 3 inches
w 8 × h 8 × d 8 centimeters

STEPHEN FABRICO
Spiral bowl

Thrown and hand-carved porcelain
Glaze and Firing: Sprayed, dipped, cone 10 firing

w 16 × h 5 × d 16 inches
w 41 × h 13 × d 41 centimeters

JOSEPH A. TRIPLO
Platter

Thrown, hand-built, molded, and cast porcelain
Glaze and Firing: Brushed, sprayed, dipped,
high-fire cone 11 firing in a gas kiln

d 15 inches
d 38 centimeters

MINAKO YAMANE-LEE
Sunset

Thrown porcelain with altered rim
Glaze and Firing: Sprayed matte
crystalline glazes, light reduction
cone 10 firing in a gas kiln

w 5 × h 4.5 × d 5 inches
w 13 × h 11 × d 13 centimeters

KATHRYN INSKEEP
Slab-built porcelain

Glaze and Firing: Soda ash, wood ash,
 volcanic ash, reduction firing

w 10 × h 13 inches
w 25 × h 33 centimeters

MEGAN HART
Teapot, cup, and saucer

Thrown and slab-built porcelain
Glaze and Firing: Painted with colored slips,
clear glaze, cone 11 gas reduction firing

w 3.5 × d 2.73 inches (cup)
w 9 × d 7 centimeters (cup)
h 7.5 inches (pot)
h 19 centimeters (pot)

GERTRUDE GRAHAM SMITH
Bowl

Thrown and altered porcelain
Glaze and Firing: Single firing to cone 10
in soda kiln

w 8 × h 6 inches
w 20 × h 15 centimeters

SANDRA BYERS
Springing #2

Thrown, pinched, cut, incised, and
extruded porcelain
Glaze and Firing: Dipped and sprayed
micro-crystalline matte glazes, cone 10
oxidation firing

w 2.25 × h 3.13 × d 2.13 inches
w 6 × h 8 × d 5 centimeters

IAN STAINTON
Altered Vase #2

Thrown and altered porcelain
Glaze and Firing: Celadon glaze, cone
10 oxidation firing

w 7 × h 12.5 inches
w 18 × h 32 centimeters

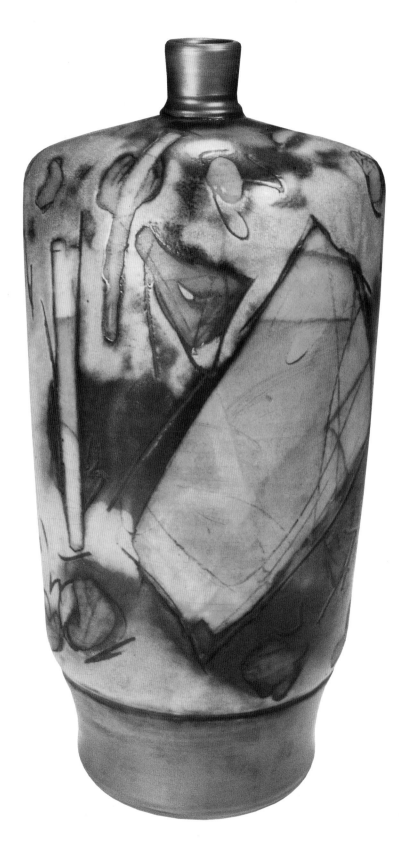

REGIS C. BRODIE
Oval bottle

Thrown and distorted porcelain
Glaze and Firing: Barry's blue glaze, wax resist,
cone 9 and 10 reduction firing

h 14 inches
h 36 centimeters

THOMAS ROHR
Salad set

Thrown porcelain
Glaze and Firing: Shino glaze,
wood firing in a kiln

w 12 × h 8 × d 4 inches
w 30 × h 20 × d 10 centimeters

DIANE KENNEY
Teapot set

Thrown porcelain
Glaze and Firing: Glazed interior,
cone 10 and cone 11 wood firing

w 8 × h 7 × d 6 inches
w 20 × h 18 × d 15 centimeters

KAREN THUESEN MASSARO
Two Nested Bowls

Thrown porcelain
Glaze and Firing: Poured interior glazes, dipped
exterior glazes, underglazes, wax resist, overglaze,
inlayed glazes, China paints, luster, bisque firing,
high-firing to cone 9-10, cone 17 oxidation
firing in an electric kiln

w 6.5 × h 4 × d 10.5 inches
w 17 × h 10 × d 27 centimeters

DONNA ANDEREGG
Sugar Jars

Thrown porcelain
Glaze and Firing: Slips, salt firing

w 5 × h 6 × d 5 inches
w 13 × h 15 × d 13 centimeters

DEANNA ECKELS
Heading Home

Thrown porcelain
Glazing and Firing: Stains, clear glaze,
underglazes, sgraffito, cone 10 reduction firing

w 18 × h 2 inches
w 46 × h 5 centimeters

EVE FLECK
Covered Bowl

Thrown porcelain with
attatched handle
Glaze and Firing: Clear glaze,
underglaze, sgraffito cone 07
oxidation firing

w 6.5 × h 8 inches
w 17 × h 20 centimeters

BERRY MATTHEWS
Grace Under Fire

Slab-built porcelain
Glaze and Firing: Cone 10 oxidation firing

w 12 × h 7 × d 6 inches
w 30 × h 18 × d 15 centimeters

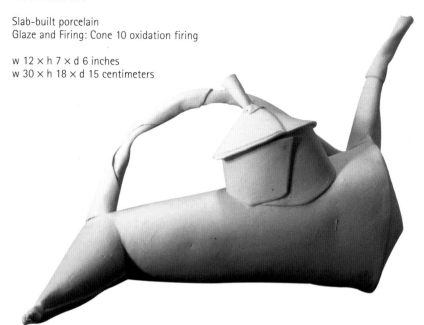

KATHRYN SHARBAUGH
Grosgrain

Hand-built porcelain
Glaze and Firing: Underglaze, clear glaze,
cone 10 oxidation firing

w 12 × h .75 × d 12 inches
w 30 × h 2 × d 30 centimeters

MARIAN BAKER
Lobster platter

Thrown and altered porcelain
Glaze and Firing: Colored slips, clear glaze,
cone 6 oxidation firing in an electric kiln

w 15 × h 2 × d 10 inches
w 38 × h 5 × d 25 centimeters

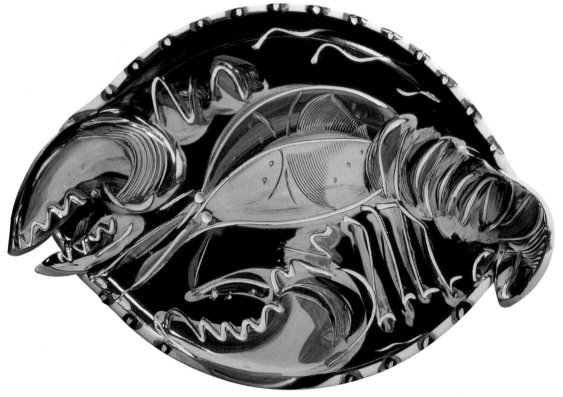

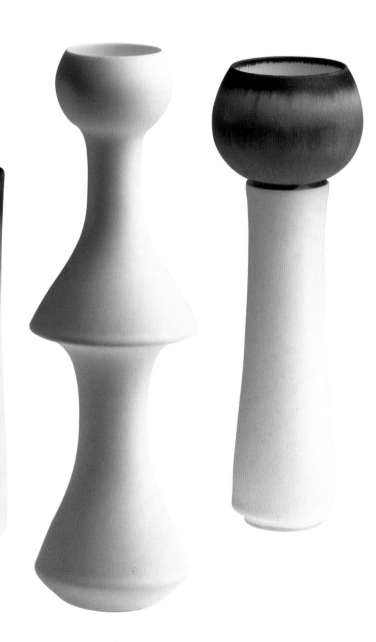

CAROLYN CHESTER
Three vases

Thrown and turned porcelain
Glaze and Firing: Slip with metal oxides under
Wollastonite glaze, cone 9 oxidation firing

w 4 × h 13 inches
w 10 × h 33 centimeters

GINA FREUEN
Cut foot-strap handled with water vessel

Thrown and hand-built porcelain
Glaze and Firing: Clear glaze over stains
and engobes, cone 5 slight-reduction firing
in a gas downdraft kiln

w 18 × h 22 × d 8 inches
w 46 × h 56 × d 20 centimeters

MARIE J. PALLUOTTO
Patchwork cup and saucer

Thrown porcelain with stamped impressions
Glaze and Firing: Incising, colored slips,
cone 10 oxidation glaze, firing in an
electric kiln

w 3 × h 4.4 × d 4 inches
w 8 × h 11 × d 10 centimeters

SUSAN MEREDITH BUNZL
Cup series

Thrown porcelain
Glaze and Firing: Barium matte glaze, black
engobe, firing at 1260°C in an electric kiln

w 6.75 × h 3.5 × d 3.25 inches
w 17 × h 9 × d 8.5 centimeters

HARRIS DELLER
Square-shaped dish with concentric arcs

Hand-built porcelain
Glaze and Firing: Incised surface, inlayed glaze,
cone 10 reduction firing

w 12 × h 3 × d 12 inches
w 30 × h 8 × d 30 centimeters

VICTORIA P. CROWELL
Looking East

Press-molded porcelain
Glaze and Firing: Hand-painted with colored
slips, cone 10 oxidation firing

w 14 × h 1 × d 17 inches
w 36 × h 3 × d 43 centimeters

155

ANDREA FÁBREGA
Ewer with Twisted Handle

Thrown porcelain
Glaze and Firing: Rutile blue with copper
red spots, high-fire reduction firing in kiln

w 1 × h 1.25 × d 1 inches
w 3 × h 4 × d 3 centimeters

DON DAVIS
Flared plate

Thrown porcelain
Glaze and Firing: Sprayed oxide, sponging,
glaze, slip trails, cone 7 light reduction firing

w 12 × h 2 × d 12 inches
w 30 × h 5 × d 30 centimeters

IRA BATES
Bowl

Thrown porcelain
Glaze and Firing: Rutile matte, cone
10 oxidation firing

w 6 × h 4 inches
w 15 × h 10 centimeters

RONALEE HERRMANN
AND ALFRED STOLKEN
Untitled

Thrown, altered, and carved porcelain
Glaze and Firing: Crystalline glaze, firing in
a modified electric kiln, gas reduction firing

h 13 x d 7 inches
h 33 x d 18 centimeters

LEAH LEITSON
Lobed sauce boat

Thrown and altered porcelain
Glaze and Firing: Salt firing

w 3.5 × h 4 × d 5 inches
w 9 × h 10 × d 13 centimeters

ALAN AND BRENDA NEWMAN
Tulip bowl

Molded and altered porcelain
Glaze and Firing: White barium matte glaze,
CuCr barium matte glaze, cone 6 oxidation
firing in an electric kiln

w 11 × h 7 inches
w 28 × h 18 centimeters

CLARK BURGAN
Ewer

Thrown stoneware
Glaze and Firing: Cone 10 soda firing

w 7 × h 15 × d 10 inches
w 18 × h × 38 d 25 centimeters

159

HUNT PROTHRO
Porcelain platter

Thrown porcelain
Glaze and Firing: Underglazes, stains,
cone 10 reduction firing

w 24 × h 4 × d 24 inches
w 61 × h 10 × d 61 inches

CHARLES B. NALLE
Half a Cup

Cast semi-vitreous, high-fire porcelain
Glaze and Firing: Layered opaque glazes,
oxidation firing

w 3 × h 3 × d 3 inches
w 8 × h 8 × d 8 centimeters

LYNN SMISER BOWERS
House platter

Slab-molded porcelain
Glaze and Firing: Cone 10 reduction glazes,
resist, oxide stains, firing to cone 10 in a
reduction atmosphere in a gas downdraft kiln

w 13 × h 10 × d 2 inches
w 33 × h 25 × d 5 centimeters

161

LOLA J. LOGSDON
#9306

Thrown and altered earthenware
Glaze and Firing: Glazes, cone 04 firing in an
electric kiln

w 7.5 × h 9.75 × d 7.5 inches
w 19 × h 25 × d 19 centimeters

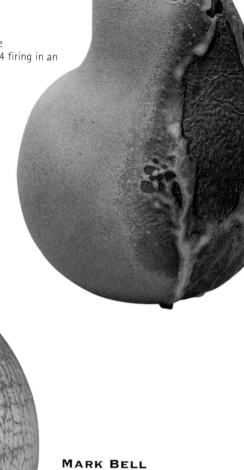

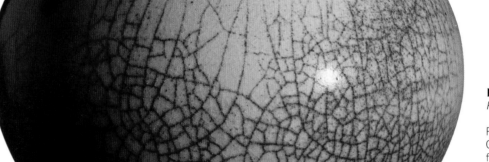

MARK BELL
Porcelain Vase #831

Porcelain
Glaze and Firing: Celadon glaze, oxidation
firing, cone 10 reduction firing

w 8 × h 8 × d 8 inches
w 20 × h 20 × d 20 centimeters

STANTON HUNTER
Craggy goblet

Thrown, slab-built, and epoxied porcelain
Glaze and Firing: Crackle glaze, smoke
cup-slip, oxides, ash glaze, luster, raku
firing on base, cone 10 reduction/luster
fire to cone 019 on base

w 3 × h 8 × d 3 inches
w 8 × h 20 × d 8 centimeters

JENNIFER A. HILL
Sugar with creamer

Thrown and ovaled porcelain
Glaze and Firing: Deep green, copper red, and
blue glaze, cone 10 reduction firing

w 4 × h 3 × d 10 inches
w 10 × h 8 × d 25 centimeters

BONNIE SEEMAN
Cup, saucer, and base

Thrown and hand-built porcelain
Glaze and Firing: Airbrushed glazes, brushed
gold luster, cone 10 oxidation firing, cone 018
gold luster firing

w 12 × h 7 × d 10 inches
w 30 × h 18 × d 25 centimeters

CAROL B. EDER
Fluid Clay series: soup bowls

Thrown and altered porcelain
Glaze and Firing: Brushed, temoku, shino, and
copper stains, firing in an anagama wood kiln

w 4 × h 7 × d 4 inches
w 10 × h 18 × d 10 centimeters

photo: Joseph Gruber

NICOLETTE MITCHELL
Up on the Horizon

Hand-built and press-molded porcelain
Glaze and Firing: Cone 03 oxidation firing in an
electric kiln

w 12 × h 11 × d 5 inches
w 30 × h 28 × d 13 centimeters

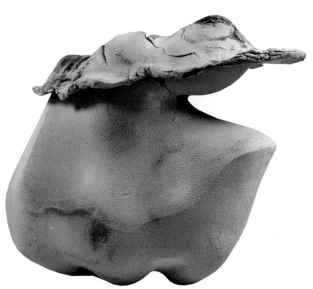

DALE HUFFMAN
Ochoko

Thrown porcelain
Glaze and Firing: Shino,
cone 9 reduction firing

w 3.39 × h 2 × d 2 inches
w 9 × h 5 × d 5 centimeters

PEG MALLOY
Square-lidded jar

Thrown and altered porcelain
Glaze and Firing: Shino slip, wood
firing in a bourry box kiln

w 6.5 × h 9.5 × d 6.5 inches
w 17 × h 24 × d 17 centimeters

LINDA ARNDT
Fairy Kaleidoscope Plate

Thrown, low-fire white ware
Glaze and Firing: Slip, underglaze, glaze,
overglaze, cone 04 multi-firing

w 25 × h 25 × d 4 inches
w 64 × h 64 × d 10 centimeters

BILLIE JEAN THEIDE
Butte #Czech 4

Slip-cast and hand-built porcelain
Glaze and Firing: Cone 15 clear glaze,
gas reduction firing, ceramic decal,
cone 015 firing in an electric kiln

w 9.5 × h 3.25 × d 2.25 inches
w 24 × h 9 × d 6 centimeters

MARIA BOFILL
Labyrinth

Hand-built porcelain
Glaze and Firing: Gas reduction
firing at 1280°C

w 14.5 × h 1.5 × d 10.25 inches
w 37 × h 4 × d 26 centimeters

NEIL PATTERSON
Set of potion bottles

Thrown and assembled porcelain
Glaze and Firing: Celadons, matte
glazes, ash glaze, cone 10 reduction
firing in a gas kiln

w 3 × h 6 × d 3 inches
w 8 × h 15 × d 8 centimeters

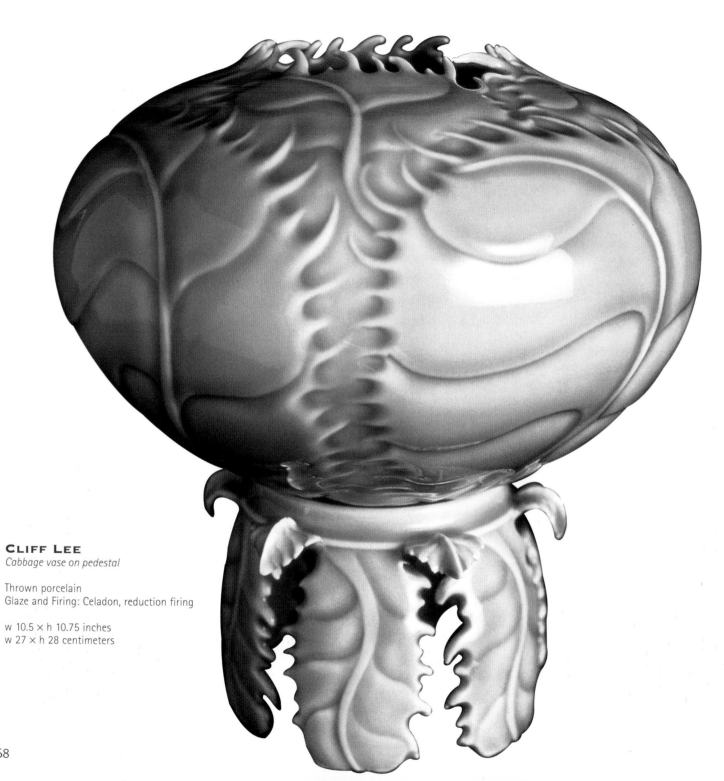

CLIFF LEE
Cabbage vase on pedestal

Thrown porcelain
Glaze and Firing: Celadon, reduction firing

w 10.5 × h 10.75 inches
w 27 × h 28 centimeters

INGRID LILLIGREN
Ruby

Thrown and altered porcelain
Glaze and Firing: Salted porcelain, cone 10
firing in an electric kiln

w 11 × h 8 × d 4 inches
w 28 × h 20 × d 10 centimeters

VINCENT SUEZ
Flight series

Thrown porcelain
Glaze and Firing: Ash glaze,
cone 12 wood firing

w 11 × h 18 × d 11 inches
w 28 × h 46 × d 28 centimeters

SHANNON NELSON
Bowl About Softness

Thrown and altered porcelaneous stoneware
Glaze and Firing: Glaze, cone 10 reduction firing

w 6.5 × h 3 × d 6 inches
w 17 × h 8 × d 15 centimeters

169

DICK LEHMAN
Thank You, Malcolm

Thrown, altered, and assembled grolleg porcelain
Glaze and Firing: Carbon-trapping glaze, cone 10
firing in a wood sagger kiln

w 5.5 × h 12.25 × d 5 inches
w 14 × h 32 × d 14 centimeters

GEOFFREY WHEELER
Teapot

Thrown, hand-built, and assembled porcelain
Glaze and Firing: Sprayed copper glazes, cone 10
soda firing

w 8 × h 9 × d 5 inches
w 20 × h 23 × d 13 centimeters

EVE FLECK
Platter

Slab-built porcelain
Glaze and Firing: Clear glaze, underglaze,
sgraffito, cone 7 oxidation firing

w 11 × h 2 × d 18 inches
w 28 × h 5 × d 46 centimeters

HIDEAKI MIYAMURA
Covered jar

Thrown porcelain
Glaze and Firing: White crackle glaze, cone 10
oxidation firing

w 12.25 × h 1 × d 12.25 inches
w 31 × h 3 × d 31 centimeters

SUSAN BEINER
Screw tea set

Molded and slip-cast porcelain
Glaze and Firing: Cone 6 oxidation, multi-firing
in gas and electric kilns

w 12 × h 21 × d 8 inches
w 30 × h 53 × d 20 centimeters

MARY T. NICHOLSON
Cup of Cups mini-series

Thrown porcelain with pulled handles
Glaze and Firing: Unglazed,
cone 6 oxidation firing

w 9.5 × h 6.5 × d 9.5 inches
w 24 × h 17 × d 24 centimeters

Stoneware is strong and opaque ceramic ware that can be gray, tan, or slightly reddish in its natural state. This high-fire, nonporous pottery is in many ways similar to porcelain. Stoneware is usually glazed pottery in which the glaze and clay have been blended together.

Ann M. Tubbs *Biscotti on Yellow Cloth*

Thrown, press-molded, and altered stoneware

Glaze and Firing: White majolica, colored stains, and glazes, oxidation firing in an electric kiln
w 8 inches
w 20 centimeters

Stoneware

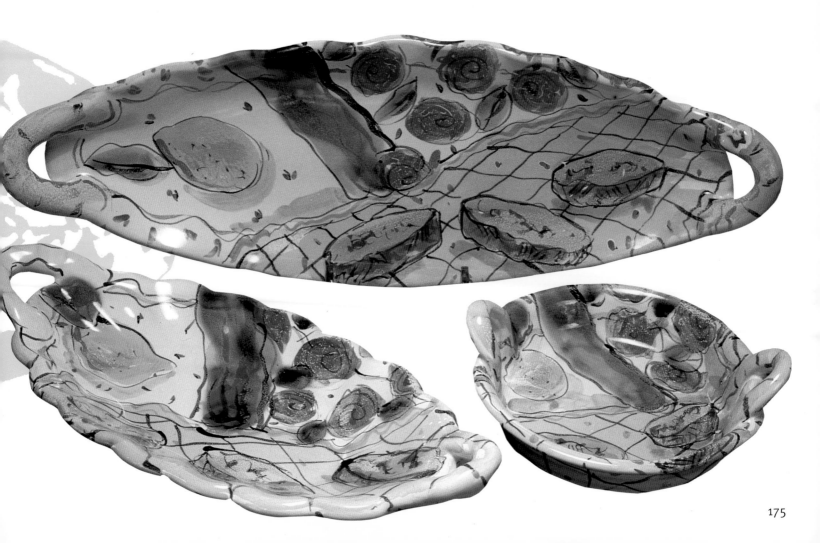

Mark Hewitt .... Dinner plate ....

Thrown stoneware

Glaze and Firing: Iron slip underglaze, shino with
blue glass, and salt glazes, wood-firing
d 11 inches
d 28 centimeters

Robert M. Winokur .... *Italian Hill Town* ...

Slab-built Pennsylvania brick clay

Glaze and Firing: Slips, engobes, and salt
glazes, salt-firing
w 40 x h 16 x d 9 inches
w 101 x h 41 x d 23 centimeters

176

Malcolm Wright ......*Rocking Vase #4* ....

Extended, altered, and assembled stoneware

Glaze and Firing: Blue china paints, wood-firing
w 9 x h 6 x d 6 inches
w 23 x h 15 x d 15 centimeters

Richard Hirsch ....*Ceremonial Cup #13* ......

Thrown and hand-built stoneware

Glaze and Firing: Terra sigillata, raku-firing
w 14.5 x h 12.5 x d 14.5 inches
w 37 x h 32 x d 37 centimeters

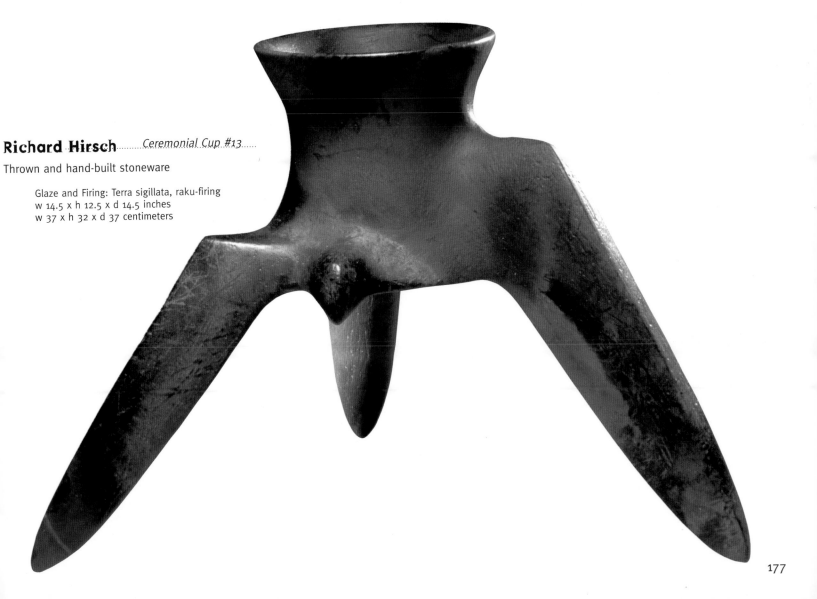

Marta Matray Gloviczki

Old Hungarian Shepherd

Hand-built stoneware

Glaze and Firing: Light oxide wash, cone 6 firing
in an electric kiln
w 8 x h 10 x d 4 inches
w 21 x h 25 x d 10 centimeters

Marl Nafziger

Fan Variation #2
platter

Thrown stoneware

Glaze and Firing: Feldspathic glaze, slip-trailed,
and sprayed glaze, cone 10 gas reduction firing
w 19 x d 1.5 inches
w 48 x d 4 centimeters

Kathleen M. Royster

Thorn Cup

Hand-built white stoneware

Glaze and Firing: Barium glaze, cone 3
oxidation firing
w 5 x h 7 inches
w 13 x h 17 centimeters

Patricia L. Hankins ·············· *Zinnia and Marigold Boxes*

Hand-built stoneware

Glaze and Firing: Copper wire and flowers for coloration, cone 07 sagger firing in gas kiln
w 6.5 x h 5 inches
w 16 x h 13 centimeters

Patricia Sannit ·········· Incised white vessel

Slab- and coil-built white stoneware

Glaze and Firing: White slip, black stain, satin glaze, cone 3 and cone 06 multi-firing in an electric kiln
w 8 x h 27.5 x d 6.5 inches
w 21 x h 70 x d 17 centimeters

Joseph G. Brown — *Figures in Boat*

Hand-built stoneware

Glaze and Firing: Copper glaze, firing in an
electric kiln
w 11 x h 12 x d 14 inches
w 28 x h 31 x d 36 centimeters

Lola J. Logsdon — #93

Thrown and altered stoneware

Glaze and Firing: Glazes, multi-firing in
electric kiln
w 8.5 x h 10 x d 9 inches
w 22 x h 25 x d 23 centimeters

Tom Maxfield — Illustrated cannister

Thrown and hand-built stoneware

Glaze and Firing: Colored slips and gunmetal
glaze, cone 6 oxidation firing
w 6 x h 12 x d 5 inches
w 15 x h 31 x d 13 centimeters

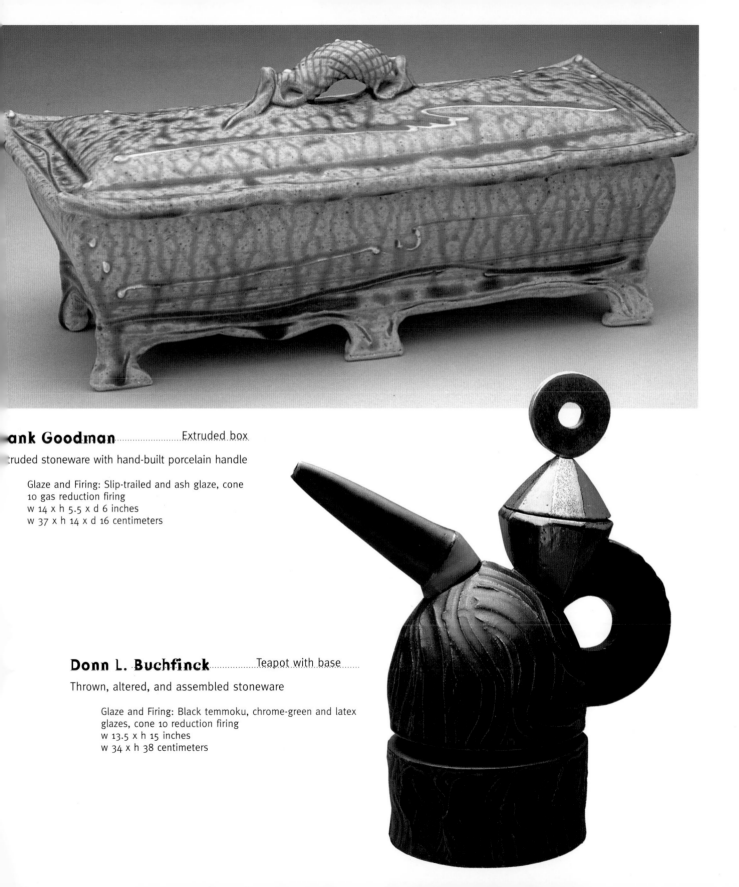

ank Goodman ....Extruded box

truded stoneware with hand-built porcelain handle

Glaze and Firing: Slip-trailed and ash glaze, cone
10 gas reduction firing
w 14 x h 5.5 x d 6 inches
w 37 x h 14 x d 16 centimeters

Donn L. Buchfinck................Teapot with base

Thrown, altered, and assembled stoneware

Glaze and Firing: Black temmoku, chrome-green and latex
glazes, cone 10 reduction firing
w 13.5 x h 15 inches
w 34 x h 38 centimeters

181

Harrison McIntosh .... *Deep Bowl*
                                      #8419

Thrown stoneware

> Photo by Schenk & Schenk
> Glaze and Firing: Black engobe and sprayed mat
> glaze, cone 5 oxidation firing
> w 12.5 x h 7.5 inches
> w 32 x h 19 centimeters

Jill Hinckley .... Set of four pitchers

Thrown stoneware

> Glaze and Firing: Temmoku glaze, high-fire
> reduction firing
> w 4 x h 4.5 x d 3 inches
> w 10 x h 11 x d 8 centimeters

Sue Nelson .... *Juno*

Hand-built stoneware

> Glaze and Firing: Sprayed low-fire glazes,
> cone 06 oxidation firing
> w 30 x h 51 x d 24 inches
> w 76 x h 130 x d 61 centimeters

R. Bruce Carpenter .... *Chawan Named*
Tide Pool

Thrown and altered stoneware

    Glaze and Firing: Shino glazes, cone 10 gas firing
    w 6 x h 3.5 inches
    w 14 x h 9 centimeters

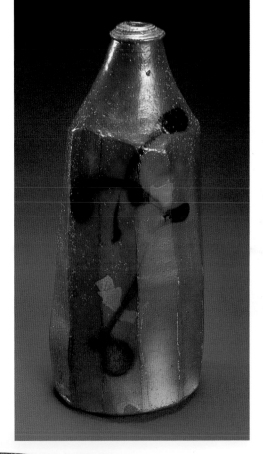

Cynthia Bringle .... *Vessel* ....

Thrown stoneware

    Glaze and Firing: Slips, wood- and salt-firing
    w 6 x h 14.5 x d 5 inches
    w 15 x h 37 x d 13 centimeters

Josh Teplitzky .... *French bread platter* ....
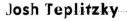

Slab-built stoneware

    Glaze and Firing: White slip and slip-trailed
    glazes, cone 10 salt-firing
    w 23 x h 1 x d 6 inches
    w 58 x h 3 x d 15 centimeters

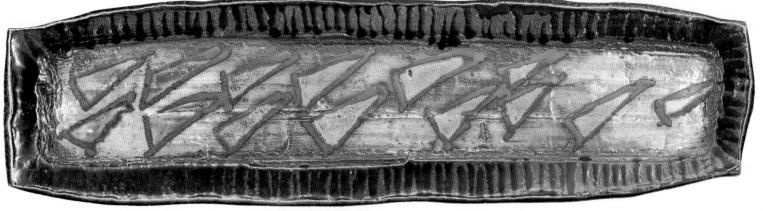

Alena Ort................*Quotation Plate:*
.................*Parables of Franz Kafka*

Hand-built stoneware

Glaze and Firing: Oxides and transparent
overglaze, low-fire firing
w 11 x h 9 x d 3 inches
w 28 x h 23 x d 8 centimeters

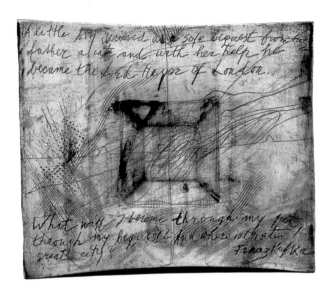

Priscilla Heep........*A King's Casserole*........

Hand-built stoneware

Glaze and Firing: Celadon glaze interior and
unglazed exterior, gas reduction firing
w 8.5 x h 8 x d 5 inches
w 22 x h 20 x d 13 centimeters

Suze Lindsay............*Pitcher and tumblers*

Thrown and assembled stoneware

Glaze and Firing: Slip and copper glazes,
salt-firing
w 14 x h 9 x d 5 inches
w 36 x h 23 x d 13 centimeters

Hsin-Chuen Lin .... Vessel ....

Thrown and altered stoneware

Glaze and Firing: Reduction glaze, cone 10
reduction firing
w 8 x h 16 x d 8 inches
w 20 x h 41 x d 20 centimeters

Catherine White .... Black bottle ....

Thrown white stoneware

Glaze and Firing: Black glaze, gas reduction firing
w 3 x h 8.5 x d 3 inches
w 8 x h 22 x d 8 centimeters

Jeremy Nudell Kalin .... Bottle ....

Thrown and altered stoneware

Glaze and Firing: Oribe glaze, firing with
cottonwood kiln
w 8 x h 15 x d 5 inches
w 20 x h 38 x d 13 centimeters

Anne Fallis-Elliott.............*Ash tea set*

Thrown, altered, and hand-built white stoneware

Glaze and Firing: Black ash glaze, cone 7 firing in
an electric kiln
Tray w 15 inches.
Tray w 38 centimeters
Teapot w 8 x h 15 inches
Teapot w 20 x h 38 centimeters

Paul Chaleff.............Cauldron with three legs

Hand-built stoneware

Glaze and Firing: Multi-layered glaze, firing
in a gas kiln
w 52 x h 30 x d 52 inches
w 132 x h 76 x d 132 centimeters

Ronald Larsen
Canister set

Thrown and altered stoneware

Glaze and Firing: Copper glaze, cone 10
reduction firing
large w 8 x h 6 x d 6 inches
large w 20 x h 15 x d 15 centimeters
medium w 8 x h 8.5 x d 6 inches
medium w 20 x h 20 x d 15 centimeters
small w 8 x h 6 x d 6 inches
small w 20 x h 15 x d 15 centimeters

Virginia Piazza
Bowl

Thrown and altered stoneware

Glaze and Firing: Shino glaze, iron slip, and
wax resist; cone 10 gas reduction firing
w 10 x h 4 x d 10 inches
w 25 x h 10 x d 25 centimeters

Lana Wilson
Ritual box

Slab-built white stoneware

Glaze and Firing: Brushed and sprayed glazes,
cone 6 and cone 06 oxidation multi-firing
w 6 x h 18 x d 6 inches
w 13 x h 46 x d 15 centimeters

Harolyn Long .... *Relief Vessel #4* ....

Slab-built white stoneware

Glaze and Firing: Clear glaze, raku-firing
w 10.5 x h 12 x d 3 inches
w 27 x h 31 x d 8 centimeters

Karen Karnes .... *Vessel* ....

Thrown and hand-built stoneware

Glaze and Firing: Glaze, wood-firing
w 17 x h 14 x d 12 inches
w 43 x h 36 x d 31 centimeters

Ken Bichell .... *Soft Belly* ....

Thrown and altered stoneware

Glaze and Firing: Ash glaze, firing in an
anagama kiln
w 10.5 x h 8.5 x d 10 inches
w 27 x h 21 x d 25 centimeters

Edith B. Murphy......Pod Grouping 3, 4, 5

Thrown, coil-built, and assembled stoneware

Glaze and Firing: Salt glazes and wax resist,
cone 08 and cone 10 multi-firing
w 32 x h 34 x d 3 inches
w 81 x h 86 x d 8 centimeters

Brad Schwieger......Salt-fired bottle

Thrown and altered stoneware

Glaze and Firing: Slips and glazes, cone 10
reduction salt-firing
w 16 x h 31 x d 9 inches
w 41 x h 79 x d 23 centimeters

189

Yoshiro Ikeda .... *Garden* ....

Coil-built stoneware

Glaze and Firing: White oracle and blue
lithium glazes, cone 09 and cone 02 oxidation
multi-firing in an electric kiln
w 14 x h 21 x d 5 inches
w 36 x h 53 x d 13 centimeters

Yoshiro Ikeda .... *Tornado* ....

Coil-built stoneware

Glaze and Firing: White oracle, green lithium, and
black glazes, oxidation firing in an electric kiln
w 16 x h 19 x d 9 inches
w 41 x h 48 x d 23 centimeters

Karen Karnes .... Vessel ....

Thrown and hand-built stoneware

Glaze and Firing: Glaze, wood-firing
w 17 x h 13 x d 13 inches
w 43 x h 33 x d 33 centimeters

Jeff Shapiro .... Vessel ....

Thrown and altered stoneware

Glaze and Firing: Natural ash-deposit glaze,
wood-firing
w 10 x h 9 x d 7 inches
w 25 x h 23 x d 18 centimeters

Dina Angel-Wing .... Square-shaped teapot

Thrown and altered stoneware

Glaze and Firing: Low-fire crackle glaze, raku-firing
w 8 x h 5 x d 6 inches
w 20 x h 13 x d 15 centimeters

John Skelton .... Teapot ....

Thrown stoneware

> Glaze and Firing: Avery slip, wood-firing
> w 10 x h 6 x d 6.5 inches
> w 25 x h 15 x d 17 centimeters

Steven Hill .... Teapot ....

Thrown, altered, and extruded stoneware

> Glaze and Firing: Slip-trailed, dipped and
> sprayed glazes, cone 10 gas reduction firing
> w 10 x h 13 x d 7 inches
> w 25 x h 33 x d 18 centimeters

Brad Schwieger .... Soda-fired vessel .....

Thrown and altered stoneware

> Glaze and Firing: Slips and glazes, cone 10
> reduction soda-firing
> w 18 x h 15 x d 7 inches
> w 46 x h 38 x d 18 centimeters

Philip Stokes *Seated Woman*

Thrown stoneware

Glaze and Firing: Wood-firing
w 7.5 x h 14 inches
w 19 x h 36 centimeters

Nicholas Joerling *Sugar bowl, creamer, and tray*

Thrown and altered stoneware

Glaze and Firing: Helix glaze over shino, wax resist,
high-fire gas reduction firing
w 3 x h 5 x d 4.5 inches
w 8 x h 13 x d 11 centimeters

Steven Hill *Cypress pitcher*

Thrown and altered stoneware

Glaze and Firing: Sprayed multi-glaze,
cone 10 gas reduction firing
w 10.5 x h 20 x d 8 inches
w 26 x h 51 x d 20 centimeters

Rimas VisGirda ...... *Smoking Blond Woman with Ponytail* teapot

Hand-built stoneware and earthenware

Glaze and Firing: Engobe, glaze, luster, pencil, and china paint, cone 10 reduction, cone 05 oxidation, cone 018 oxidation multi-firing
w 11 x h 9 x d 5 inches
w 28 x h 23 x d 13 centimeters

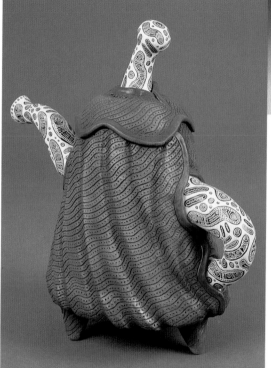

Marko Fields .... *I'm a Little Teapot, Not Too Short, Pretty Stout with Tattoos*

Hand-built, thrown, and carved stoneware with porcelain handle, spout, and finial

Glaze and Firing: Incised underglaze on porcelain, underglazed/glazed stoneware, cone 6 oxidation firing
w 16 x h 15 x d 8 inches
w 41 x h 38 x d 20 centimeters

Linda Fribley .... *Spirits of the Past*

Hand-built stoneware

Glaze and Firing: Porcelain slip, red iron oxide and copper wash, cone 7 reduction firing
w 16.5 x h 10 x d 7.5 inches
w 42 x h 25 x d 19 centimeters

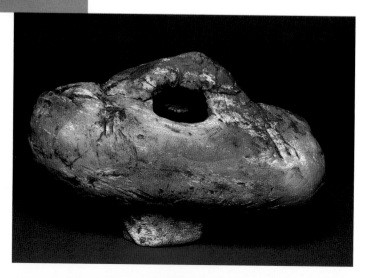

Fred Johnston .... *Zoomorphic Teapot* *No #1*

Hand-built and thrown stoneware

Glaze and Firing: light salt glaze, white slip with black slip decoration, cone 10 light salt oxidation firing
w 10 x h 7 inches
w 25.5 x h 18 centimeters

Michael Chipperfield .... Ewer

Hand-built and thrown stoneware

Glaze and Firing: Manganese/copper glaze exterior, cone 6 gas reduction firing
w 12 x h 9.5 x d 4.5 inches
w 31 x h 24 x d 11 centimeters

thi Jefferson .... Sugar bowl and creamer

wn and altered stoneware

Glaze and Firing: Terra sigillata, metallic oxides, slip, and porcelain oils, gas salt-firing
Creamer w 3 x h 3.5 inches
Creamer w 8 x h 9 centimeters
Sugar bowl w 3 x h 3 inches
Sugar bowl w 8 x h 8 centimeters

Mark D. Derby .... *Nola #2* ....

Slab-built, press-molded, and extruded terra cotta

Glaze and Firing: Crackle slip and sprayed glaze, cone 03 and cone 06 oxidation firing in an electric kiln
w 13 x h 11 x d 5 inches
w 28 x h 24 x d 11 centimeters

Ana Varela .... Cookie jar ....

Thrown stoneware

Glaze and Firing: Slips and glazes, cone 7 oxidation firing
w 12 x h 18 x d 8 inches
w 31 x h 46 x d 20 centimeters

Bruce A. Barry .... *Journey Entry #33* ....

Thrown and altered stoneware

Glaze and Firing: Glaze and oxide wash, gas reduction and electric multi-firing
h 10 x d 6 inches
h 25 x d 15 centimeters

Steffanie Samuels .... *Indigo Sky* plate .....

Coil-built stoneware

> Glaze and Firing: Porcelain slip, glaze, and oil
> paint, cone 8 oxidation firing in an electric kiln
> w 23 x d 7 inches
> w 58 x d 18 centimeters

Alleghany Meadows .... Sugar bowl ....
.... and creamer set ....

Thrown, altered, and assembled white stoneware

> Glaze and Firing: Soda glaze exterior and amber liner,
> cone 10 soda firing
> w 11 x h 4 inches
> w 28 x h 10 centimeters

Susan Beecher .... Three oval jars ....

Thrown and altered stoneware

> Glaze and Firing: Shino, temmoku, and copper
> mat glazes, cone 10 gas reduction firing
> w 6 x h 12 x d 5 inches
> w 15 x h 31 x d 13 centimeters

Jason Hess .... Bo

Thrown stoneware

Glaze and Firing: Ash glaze, wood-firin
w 6.5 x h 3.5 inches
w 17 x h 9 centimeters

Michael Cohen .... Architectural teapot

Hand-built and extruded stoneware

Glaze and Firing: Dipped blue glaze,
cone 10 gas reduction
w 3 x h 7 x d 18 inches
w 8 x h 18 x d 46 centimeters

Bill Griffith......Teapot.......................

Slab-built stoneware

Glaze and Firing: Natural wood-ash glaze and
flashing slip, cone 10 firing in an anagama kiln
w 11 x h 11 x d 5 inches
w 28 x h 28 x d 13 centimeters

Chuck Solberg.......Tea jug.....................

Thrown, altered, and faceted stoneware

Glaze and Firing: Low-fire slips, cone 10
sagger firing
w 10 x h 12 inches
w 25 x h 31 centimeters

Hanna Lore Hombordy...Four Pods......

Hand-built white stoneware

Glaze and Firing: Black underglaze, satin clear
glaze, black gloss glaze interior, cone 5 and cone
04 firing in an electric kiln
w 4 x h 2 x d 10 inches
w 10 x h 5 x d 25 centimeters

Ragnar Naess................Candle.stands................

Thrown, reformed, carved, incised, and
constructed stoneware

> Glaze and Firing: Thin oxide washes and glazes,
> cone 6 gas oxidation firing
> w 7.5 x h 23 x d 7.5 inches
> w 18 x h 58 x d 18 centimeters

Jared Jaffe................Teapots................

Cast and hand-built stoneware

> Glaze and Firing: High-fire gloss glazes, cone 6
> firing in an electric kiln
> w 10 x h 12 x d 6 inches
> w 25 x h 31 x d 15 centimeters

Steve Davis-Rosenbaum................Covered................
jar set

Thrown stoneware

> Glaze and Firing: Salt glaze, gas firing
> w 13 x h 8.5 x d 5 inches
> w 33 x h 22 x d 13 centimeters

Makoto Yabe .... *Two* ....

Thrown and coil-built stoneware

Glaze and Firing: Colored slips and
glazes, cone 10 reduction firing
w 8 x h 16 x d 12 inches
w 20 x h 41 x d 31 centimeters

Bruce M. Winn .... *Cup and saucer* ....

Slab-built white stoneware

Glaze and Firing: Inlaid high-fire glazes with wax
resist, cone 10 oxidation firing in an electric kiln
w 6 x h 4 x d 4.5 inches
w 15 x h 10 x d 11 centimeters

Makoto Yabe .... *Vessel* ....

Thrown and coil-built stoneware

Glaze and Firing: Colored slips and
glazes, cone 8 reduction firing
w 16 x h 39 x d 16 inches
w 41 x h 99 x d 41 centimeters

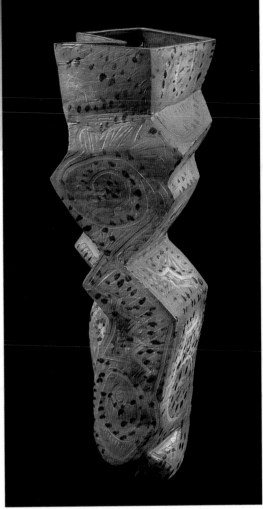

Martha Sifnas .... *Birdbath #1*

Slab-built and slump-molded stoneware

Glaze and Firing: Sprayed and poured shino and oribe glazes, cone 10 gas reduction firing
w 18 x h 8 inches
w 46 x h 20 centimeters

Barbara Knutson .... Vase

Hand-built white stoneware

Glaze and Firing: Sprayed glazes, cone 11 reduction firing
w 7 x h 9 x d 3.5 inches
w 18 x h 23 x d 9 centimeters

Bruce M. Winn............Teapot.........

Slab-built white stoneware

Glaze and Firing: Inlaid high-fire glazes with
wax resist, cone 10 oxidation firing in an
electric kiln
w 13 x h 13 x d 7 inches
w 33 x h 33 x d 18 centimeters

Lisa Yu ....*Dancing* teapot...........

Thrown and assembled stoneware

Glaze and Firing: Engobe and glaze
w 15 x h 18 x d 11 inches
w 38 x h 46 x d 28 centimeters

Erica Wurtz.................*Ruffle* platter...........

Thrown and hand-built stoneware

Glaze and Firing: White slip and glazes, cone
9/10 reduction firing
w 20 x h 7 x d 8 inches
w 51 x h 18 x d 20 centimeters

Rebecca Plummer and Jon Ellenbogen

Soup tureen, bowls and ladle

Thrown, extruded, and hand-built stoneware

Glaze and Firing: Slip and glaze, reduction firing
w 9 x h 9 inches
w 23 x h 23 centimeters

Warren Frederick

Storage jar without neck

Coil-built, altered, and thrown stoneware

Glaze and Firing: Ash glaze, firing in an anagama kiln
w 21 x h 25.5 x d 21 inches
w 53 x h 65 x d 53 centimeters

Danny Sheu .... Vessel ....

Thrown, altered, and assembled stoneware

Glaze and Firing: Barium blue glaze, cone 10
reduction firing
w 8 x h 21 x d 6 inches
w 20 x h 53 x d 15 centimeters

Anne Goldman .... *Strata Dance*

Thrown and hand-built stoneware

Glaze and Firing: Glazed interior, porcelain- and
iron-slip exterior, high-fire firing
w 22 x h 6.5 inches
w 56 x h 17 centimeters

Louise Harter .... Juicer ....

Thrown and carved stoneware

Glaze and Firing: Copper glaze interior, wood
and salt multi-firing
w 7 x h 4 x d 4.5 inches
w 18 x h 10 x d 12 centimeters

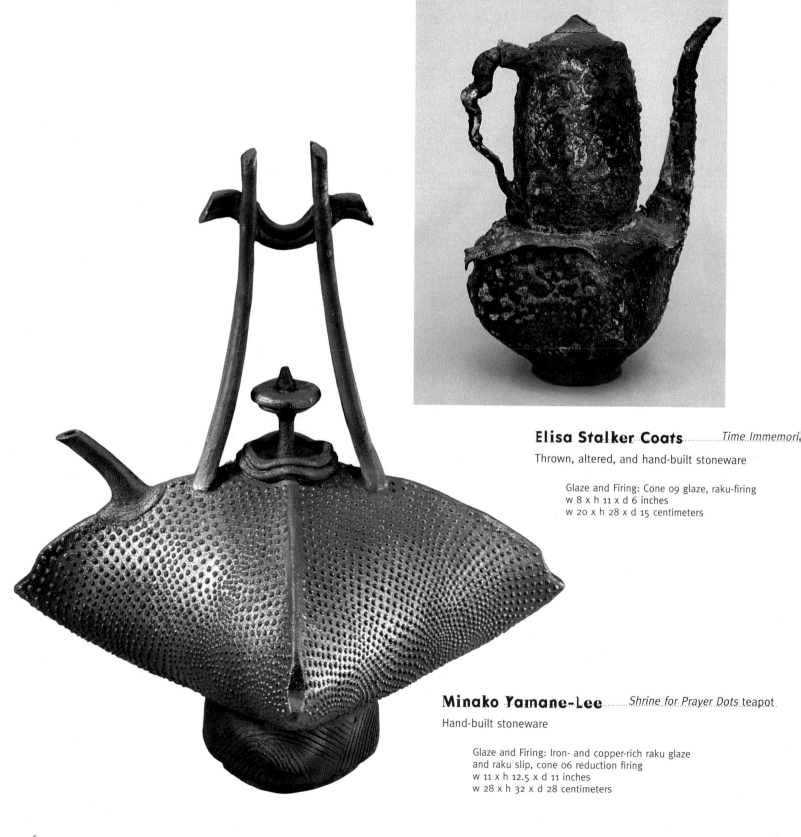

Elisa Stalker Coats...............*Time Immemori*

Thrown, altered, and hand-built stoneware

Glaze and Firing: Cone 09 glaze, raku-firing
w 8 x h 11 x d 6 inches
w 20 x h 28 x d 15 centimeters

Minako Yamane-Lee..........*Shrine for Prayer Dots* teapot

Hand-built stoneware

Glaze and Firing: Iron- and copper-rich raku glaze
and raku slip, cone 06 reduction firing
w 11 x h 12.5 x d 11 inches
w 28 x h 32 x d 28 centimeters

Hiroshi Ikehata .... *Crevices vase*

Hand-built stoneware

Glaze and Firing: Glaze, firing in an anagama kiln
w 18 x h 14.5 x d 5 inches
w 46 x h 37 x d 13 centimeters

Robert Turner .... *Black Mountain Note*

Thrown and altered stoneware

Glaze and Firing: Iron- and zinc-rich glaze,
reduction firing
w 15.5 x h 16.5 inches
w 39 x h 42 centimeters

Robert Turner .... *Akan V*

Thrown and altered stoneware

Glaze and Firing: Iron- and zinc-rich
glaze, reduction firing
w 15.5 x h 21 inches
w 39 x h 53 centimeters

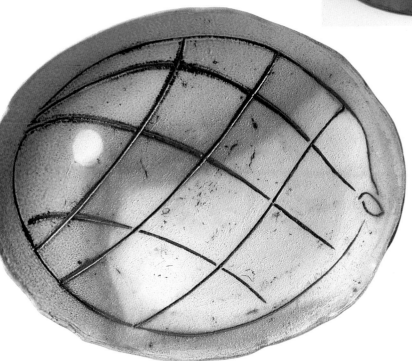

Clark Burgan .... *Plate*

Molded stoneware

Glaze and Firing: Salt glaze, cone 8
reduction firing
w 14 x d 12 inches
w 36 x d 31 centimeters

James G. Robertson .... *Tenuous* teapot ......

Thrown, altered, and assembled white stoneware

Glaze and Firing: Sprayed low-fire mat glaze,
cone 2, cone 06 multi-firing in an electric kiln
w 6 x h 12 x d 15 inches
w 15 x h 31 x d 38 centimeters

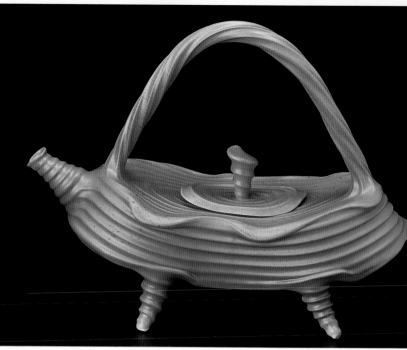

Nancy J. Utterback .... Large platter #3 ─
Journal series

Thrown stoneware

Glaze and Firing: Slips and overglaze,
cone 10 salt-firing
w 5 x h 8 inches
w 13 x h 20 centimeters

Richard T. Notkin *Hexagonal Curbside Teapot—Variation #17* from *Yixing* series

Molded and slip-cast stoneware

> Glaze and Firing: Unglazed, oxidation firing in an electric kiln
> w 8 x h 5 x d 4 inches
> w 20 x h 13 x d 10 centimeters

Avra Leodas Large green oval vessel

Coil-built stoneware

> Glaze and Firing: Sprayed glaze, cone 7 reduction firing
> w 25.5 x h 16 x d 13 inches
> w 65 x h 41 x d 33 centimeters

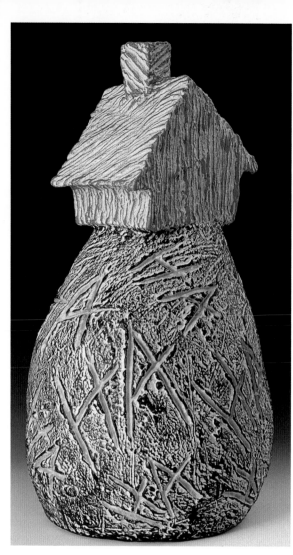

John McCuistion ....._Island Home_ bottle......

Hand-built stoneware

> Glaze and Firing: Slip glazes, cone 7 firing in an
> electric kiln
> w 11 x h 20 x d 11 inches
> w 28 x h 51 x d 28 centimeters

Patrick S. Crabb ....._Lucky Fortune_..........

Slab-built and slump-molded stoneware

> Glaze and Firing: Cone 04 glazes, cone 02 firing
> in an electric kiln
> w 27 inches
> w 69 centimeters

Harvey Sadow
Vessel from *Jupiter Diary* series

Thrown stoneware

Glaze and Firing: Eutectic slips, raku-firing and reduction firing
w 13 x h 10.5 inches
w 33 x h 27 centimeters

Paul A. Menchhofer
Aurora

Thrown stoneware

Glaze and Firing: Sprayed raku glazes, raku multi-firings
h 48 x d 27 inches
h 122 x d 69 centimeters

Lanse Stover
Teapot with indigo terra sigillata and red knob

Slab-built stoneware

Glaze and Firing: Glaze interior, sprayed soda-ash, china paint, and terra sigillata exterior, cone 6 gas and cone 018 electric multi-firing
w 12 x h 12 x d 2.5 inches
w 31 x h 31 x d 6 centimeters

Walter Dexter .... *Red Dot in Black Landscape*

Coil-built stoneware

Glaze and Firing: Chrome-red glaze and black and brown slips, cone 6 gas and cone 08 electric multi-firing
w 19 x h 24 x d 4 inches
w 47 x h 60 x d 10 centimeters

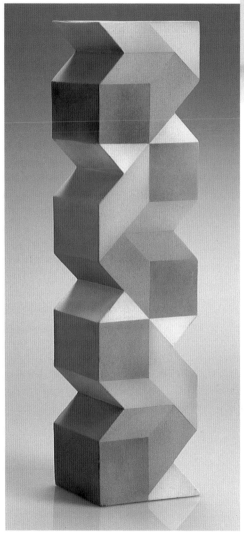

Yvonne Kleinveld .... *Dimension vase*

Slab-built stoneware

Glaze and Firing: Glaze interior, colored slip exterior, cone 4 gas multi-firing
w 4 x h 18 x d 4 inches
w 10 x h 45 x d 10 centimeters

Robert Sanderson .... Platter

Thrown stoneware

Glaze and Firing: White slip, cone 11 wood-firin
w 12 inches
w 31 centimeters

Tineke van Gils .... *Woman with Three Legs*

Thrown stoneware

Glaze and Firing: Poured glaze, cone 6
oxidation firing
w 15 x h 24 x d 15 inches
w 36 x h 60 x d 36 centimeters

Jim Leedy .... Plate

Thrown and hand-built stoneware

Photo courtesy of Leedy Voulkos
Gallery
Glaze and Firing: Low-fire glaze, firing
in an anagama kiln and gas kiln
w 18.5 x h 18.5 x d 3.5 inches
w 47 x h 47 x d 9 centimeters

Paulien Ploeger .... Looper

Thrown, reconstructed, stacked, and
assembled stoneware

Glaze and Firing: Brushed colored slips
with paper resist, salt glaze, cone 10 gas
reduction firing
h 12 inches
h 30 centimeters

D. Leslie Ferst ···················· *Grotto 40* ·······

Hand-built, carved, and assembled stoneware

Photo by Ken Burns
Glaze and Firing: Underglaze, slips, and glaze,
cone 9 reduction firing
w 18 x h 52 x d 16 inches
w 46 x h 132 x d 41 centimeters

Robert Barron ···························· *Jar* ·······

Thrown and coil-built stoneware

Glaze and Firing: Shino glaze, wood-firing
in nabori-gama kiln
w 19.5 x h 28 inches
w 50 x h 72 centimeters

Shiko Otani ·············· *Shictaraki vase* ··············

Thrown stoneware

Glaze and Firing: Unglazed, wood-firing
w 10.5 x h 10 x d 10.5 inches
w 27 x h 25 x d 27 centimeters

Bill Rowland *Motion bowl*

Thrown and altered stoneware

Glaze and Firing: Slips, glaze, and sprayed oxide, salt-firing
h 5 x d 8.5 inches
h 13 x d 21 centimeters

Hugo X. Velásquez *Tea bowl*

Thrown stoneware

Glaze and Firing: Glaze, cone 9 reduction firing
w 3.5 x h 3 inches
w 9 x h 8 centimeters

Joseph W. Bennion *Cup and saucer*

Thrown stoneware

Glaze and Firing: Slips, salt-firing and cone 10 gas firing
w 6 x h 3.5 inches
w 15 x h 9 centimeters

arbara Tipton *Red and Green*

rown, cut, altered, and assembled stoneware

Glaze and Firing: Slips and glazes, multi-firing in an electric kiln
w 13 x h 7 x d 4 inches
w 33 x h 18 x d 10 centimeters

Martin Möhwald............Platter..

Thrown stoneware

Glaze and Firing: Black slips, cone 5
firing in an electric kiln
d 43 inches
d 109 centimeters

Ellen Shankin.............................Tureen...........

Thrown stoneware

Glaze and Firing: Satin black glaze and sprayed
slip glaze, cone 9 reduction firing
w 14 x h 8 inches
w 36 x h 20 centimeters

John Chalke
Thrown and texturized bowl

Thrown stoneware

Glaze and Firing: Multi-glaze, firing in an electric kiln
w 8.5 x h 5.5 inches
w 22 x h 14 centimeters

Cathi Jefferson
Teapot

Thrown and altered stoneware

Glaze and Firing: Terra sigillata, metallic oxides, slips, and porcelain oils, gas salt-firing
w 3.5 x h 8 inches
w 9 x h 20 centimeters

Richard Milgrim
Chosen Garatsu Faceted Water Jar— Mentori Mizuashi

Thrown, faceted, and paddled red stoneware

Glaze and Firing: Poured ash- and iron-saturate glazes, high-fire oxidation wood-firing
w 6.5 x h 7 x d 6 inches
w 17 x h 18 x d 16 centimeters

Jeff Oestreich .... Beaked pitcher ....

Thrown and altered stoneware

Glaze and Firing: Copper glaze, cone 10 soda-
and salt-firing
w 12 x h 10 x d 4 inches
w 30 x h 25 x d 10 centimeters

Dan Edmunds .... Cruet ......

Hand-built stoneware

Glaze and Firing: Wood-firing
w 11 x h 11 x d 2.5 inches
w 28 x h 28 x d 6 centimeters

John Parker Glick .... Plate

Thrown stoneware

Glaze and Firing: Slips, brushed glazes, color
washes, and wax resist, reduction firing
w 23 inches
w 58 centimeters

Ka-kwong Hui .... Covered jar ....

Thrown and hand-built stoneware

Glaze and Firing: Glaze, firing in an electric kiln
w 7 x h 10 x d 5 inches
w 18 x h 25 x d 13 centimeters

Kathryn Finnerty .... Pitcher ....

Thrown, altered, and constructed stoneware

Glaze and Firing: Shino and ash glazes,
cone 10 wood-firing
w 3 x h 11 x d 5 inches
w 9 x h 28 x d 13 centimeters

Hilda Merom .... Sagger Pot #2 ......

Thrown and altered stoneware

Glaze and Firing: Unglazed, cone 2 gas reduction
sagger firing
w 8.5 x h 10.5 inches
w 21 x h 26 centimeters

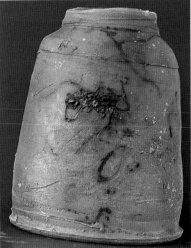

Steve Tomaszewski .... Covered dish for sweets

Thrown and trimmed white stoneware

Glaze and Firing: Unglazed, sagger firing
w 10 x h 6.5 inches
w 25 x h 15 centimeters

Mercedes Alabern .... Vessel ....

Thrown and slab-built stoneware

Glaze and Firing: Brushed slips, glazes,
and lusters, cone 9 reduction multi-firing
w 10 x h 16 x d 4 inches
w 26 x h 42 x d 10 centimeters

Hiroshi Nakayama .... *Ceremonial* vessel

Thrown and slab-built stoneware

Glaze and Firing: Wood-ash glazes, reduction multi-firing
w 11.5 x h 3.5 x d 11.5 inches
w 29 x h 9 x d 29 centimeters

Jane Morse .... *Ram vessel*

Hand-built and assembled stoneware

Glaze and Firing: Sprayed slip, wood-firing
w 8 x h 16 x d 6 inches
w 20 x h 40 x d 15 centimeters

Christopher Gustin .... *Spittoon*

Thrown and hand-built stoneware

Glaze and Firing: Wood-ash glaze, high-fire reduction firing
w 16 x h 15 x d 15 inches
w 41 x h 38 x d 38 centimeters

Christopher Gustin .... Teapot ....

Thrown and hand-built stoneware

Glaze and Firing: Salt glaze, high-fire salt firing
w 13 x h 12 x d 7 inches
w 33 x h 31 x d 18 centimeters

on Reitz ...... *In Celebration of Vessel* ....

rown stoneware

Glaze and Firing: Wood-ash glaze, firing in an
anagama kiln
w 14 x h 26 inches
w 36 x h 66 centimeters

Don Reitz .... *Emergence* ....

Slab- and coil-built stoneware

Glaze and Firing: Wood-ash glaze, firing in an
anagama kiln
w 16 x h 36 inches
w 41 x h 91 centimeters

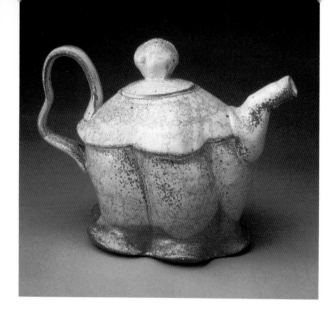

Lisa Stinson *Montana teapot*

Thrown and altered white stoneware

Glaze and Firing: Unglazed, wood- and salt-firing
w 12 x h 9 x d 5 inches
w 30 x h 23 x d 13 centimeters

Matt Wilt *Relic*

Slip-cast and assembled stoneware

Glaze and Firing: Slip-glazes,
reduction firing
w 18 x h 8 x d 5 inches
w 46 x h 20 x d 12 centimeters

Matt Wilt *Funnels*

Slip-cast and assembled stoneware

Glaze and Firing: Slips, reduction firing
w 21 x h 10 x d 5 inches
w 33 x h 26 x d 13 centimeters

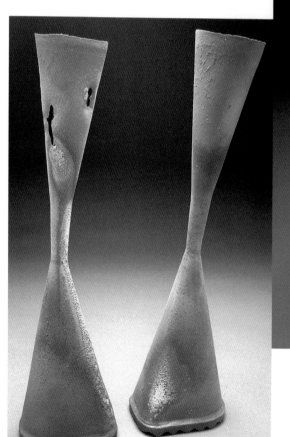

Margaret McCaul *Rainbow Lorikeet*
from *Tucker Box* series

Thrown and hand-built stoneware

Glaze and Firing: Majolica and brushed glaze, cone 4
oxidation firing in an electric kiln
w 12 x h 12 x d 7 inches
w 30 x h 30 x d 18 centimeters

Robin Johnson *Inner Shell*

Hand-built stoneware

Glaze and Firing: Firing in an anagama kiln
w 7 x h 17.5 x d 13 inches
w 18 x h 40 x d 33 centimeters

Ruthanne Tudball........Oval teapot.... on four feet

Thrown stoneware

Glaze and Firing: Slip- and soda-glazes, cone 10
gas reduction firing
w 5.5 x h 9 x d 4.5 inches
w 14 x h 22 x d 11 centimeters

Dong Hee Suh........*Transfiguration on the* *Mountain 3*

Hand-built stoneware

Glaze and Firing: Low-fire glazes, cone 04 firing
w 15 x h 36 x d 8 inches
w 37 x h 89 x d 20 centimeters

John H. Leach .... Bottles ....

Thrown stoneware

Glaze and Firing: Feldspathic glazes,
cone 10 wood sagger-firing
h 10 inches
h 25 centimeters

Carolyn Fortney .... *Radiance* ....

Hand-built stoneware

Glaze and Firing: Slips and stains, cone 5 gas
reduction firing
w 12 x h 13 x d 7 inches
w 31 x h 33 x d 18 centimeters

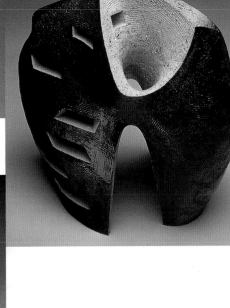

Bacia Edelman .... *Lichen* teapot ....

Hand-built and slab-built stoneware

Glaze and Firing: Slip, underglaze, crushed glaze,
and sprayed lichen glaze; cone 06 and cone 6
multi-firing in an electric kiln
w 12 x h 9.5 x d 3 inches
w 31 x h 25 x d 8 centimeters

WINTHROP BYERS
Copper Red Platter #3

Thrown stoneware
Glaze and Firing: Airbrushed iron and
copper glazes, cone 11 reduction firing
in natural gas ceramic fiber kiln

w 15 × h 1.5 inches
w 38 × h 4 centimeters

RONALD LARSEN
Sake set

Thrown, altered, and fluted stoneware
Glaze and Firing: Ash-like copper glaze,
cone 10 firing

w 5 × h 5 × d 6 inches
w 13 × h 13 × d 15 centimeters

RIMAS VISGIRDA
Smoking Woman with Baseball Cap Teapot

Thrown and altered stoneware
Glaze and Firing: Cone 10 oxidation firing, cone
10 engobes, cone 05 pencil glazes, cone 018
glaze, lusters, cone 05 oxidation firing, cone
018 oxidation firing

w 9 × h 9 × d 5 inches
w 23 × h 23 × d 13 centimeters

CATHERINE WHITE
Plate with glass pattern

Thrown white stoneware
Glaze and Firing: White slip, iron brushwork,
celadon glaze, gas firing

w 11 × h 1.5 × d 11 inches
w 28 × h 4 × d 28 centimeters

STEVEN HILL
Cypress ewer

Thrown and altered stoneware body with pulled
handle and spout
Glaze and Firing: Sprayed glazes, cone 10 gas
reduction firing

w 11 × h 19 × d 7 inches
w 28 × h 48 × d 18 centimeters

DAN EDMUNDS
Teapot

Hand-built stoneware
Glaze and Firing: Slips, black glaze, wood
firing with salt

w 2 × h 9 × d 7 inches
w 5 × h 23 × d 18 centimeters

BILL GRIFFITH
Oval casserole

Thrown and altered stoneware
Glaze and Firing: Shino glazed interior,
natural ash glazed exterior, firing in an
anagama wood kiln

w 12 × h 5 × d 6 inches
w 30 × h 13 × d 15 centimeters

DAN FINNEGAN
Mug

Thrown stoneware
Glaze and Firing: Ash glaze, crackle slip,
wood fired with light salt

w 4 × h 5 × d 4 inches
w 10 × h 13 × d 10 centimeters

DICK LEHMAN
Whiskey for Three

Thrown and altered stoneware
Glaze and Firing: Natural ash glaze,
cone 12 wood firing

w 3.25 × h 4 × d 2.5 inches
w 9 × h 10 × d 6 centimeters

NANCY BARBOUR
Catfish coffee server

Thrown stoneware
Glaze and Firing: Slip, washes, soda,
wood firing

w 7 × h 8 × d 4 inches
w 18 × h 20 × d 10 centimeters

BRAD SCHWIEGER
Slab-fired teapot

Thrown and altered stoneware body with
press-molded spout and handle
Glaze and Firing: Salt glaze, slips,
cone 9 reduction firing with salt

w 11 × h 23 × d 6 inches
w 28 × h 58 × d 15 centimeters

D. LESLIE FERST
Grotto 43 series

Hand-built, carved, and assembled stoneware
Glaze and Firing: Underglaze engobes
and glaze wash, cone 9 reduction firing

w 26 × h 42 × d 26 inches
w 66 × h 107 × d 66 centimeters

MIKA NEGISHI
Me, Myself, and I

Hand-built stoneware
Glaze and Firing: Sprayed cone 1 glazes,
firing in an electric kiln

w 16 × h 24 × d 13 inches
w 41 × h 61 × d 33 centimeters

RAGNAR NAESS
Chinese bud vase

Thrown, slab-incised, constructed, and carved
stoneware
Glaze and Firing: Oxidation firing in gas and
electric kilns

w 4.5 × h 10.25 × d 4.5 inches
w 11 × h 26 × d 11 centimeters

PAUL A. MENCHHOFER
Water Jar

Thrown stoneware
Glaze and Firing: Sprayed multiple
raku glazes, multi-firing in a raku car kiln

h 21 × d 28 inches
h 53 × d 71 centimeters

LEN EICHLER
Pile-up

Thrown stoneware assembled in mold
Glaze and Firing: Iron oxide stain,
cone 6 oxidation firing

w 6 × h 9 × d 6 inches
w 15 × h 23 × d 15 centimeters

HWANG JENG-DAW
Teapots: Functionally Old Couple

Hand-built, thrown, and altered stoneware
Glaze and Firing: Unglazed, cone 8
oxidation firing

w 15 × h 15 × d 12 inches
w 38 × h 38 × d 30 centimeters

KEN BICHELL
Thrown stoneware

Glaze and Firing: Fly ash glaze,
seven-day firing in an anagama
wood kiln

w 15 × h 10 × d 1 inches
w 38 × h 25 × d 3 centimeters

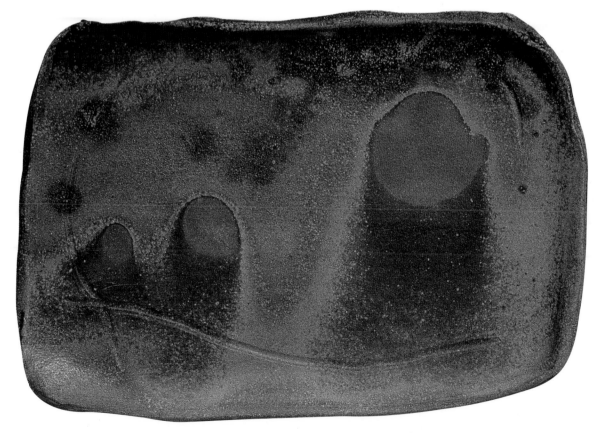

MATT WILT
Sustain

Slip-cast and hand-built stoneware
Glaze and Firing: Slips, high-fire
reduction firing

w 10 × h 9 × d 5 inches
w 25 × h 23 × d 13 centimeters

ARDIS BOURLAND
Cream pitcher

Thrown stoneware
Glaze and Firing: Cone 9 reduction firing

w 6 × h 5.5 × d 3.25 inches
w 15 × h 14 × d 8.5 centimeters

YVONNE KLEINVELD
S-vase

Stoneware
Glaze and Firing: Sinter engobe exterior; glazed
interior, firing to 1160˚C in a gas kiln

w 4 × h 12 × d 4 inches
w 10 × h 30 × d 10 cm

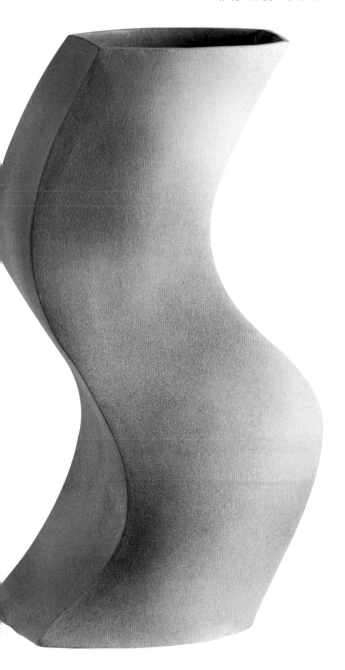

PAUL HEROUX
4

Thrown porcelaneous stoneware
Glaze and Firing: Cone 10 glazes and oxides, wax
resist, cone 10 reduction firing

w 22 × h 5 × d 22 inches
w 56 × h 13 × d 56 centimeters

BRUCE M. WINN
Bottle form

Slab-built white stoneware
Glaze and Firing: Wax resist, inlayed glaze,
cone 10 oxidation firing in an electric kiln

w 10 × h 24 × d 10 inches
w 25 × h 61 × d 25 centimeters

SAM TAYLOR
Pocketbook Teapot with Square Cups

Thrown and altered stoneware
Glaze and Firing: Copper glaze, wood firing

w 6 × h 12 × d 2 inches
w 15 × h 30 × d 5 centimeters

JEFF OESTREICH
Beaked pitcher

Thrown stoneware
Glaze and Firing: Dipped, salt glazed

w 10 × h 10 × d 4 inches
w 25 × h 25 × d 10 centimeters

FRANK PITCHER
Pitcher

Thrown and altered stoneware
with pulled handle
Glaze and Firing: Slip, gray liner glaze,
cone 10 salt firing

w 6.5 × h 7.5 × d 5 inches
w 17 × h 19 × d 13 centimeters

GEORGE BAKER
Frog Teapot 1

Thrown and hand-built stoneware
Glaze and Firing: Oxide colored slips,
oxidation firing

w 14 × h 24 × d 8 inches
w 36 × h 61 × d 20 centimeters

JOHN KANTAR
Bird pitcher

Thrown, altered, and hand-built stoneware
Glaze and Firing: Sgraffito, engobe,
soda, gas firing

w 10.5 × h 9 × d 6.75 inches
w 27 × h 23 × d 18 centimeters

HILDA MEROM
Sagger plate

Thrown and altered stoneware
Glaze and Firing: Unglazed, cone 2
reduction firing in a gas sagger kiln

d 18.5 inches
d 47 centimeters

241

ROBERT WOO
Teapot

Thrown and assembled stoneware
Glaze and Firing: Layered glazes, trailed and
brushed glazes and washes, reduction firing

w 9 × h 11 inches
w 23 × h 28 centimeters

**MICHAEL G. ROSEBERRY AND
BRUCE M. WINN**
Cup and saucers

Slab-built white stoneware
Glaze and Firing: Cone 6 oxidation firing in an
electric kiln

w 7 × h 4 × d 5 inches
w 18 × h 10 × d 13 centimeters

STEFFANIE SAMUELS
Leaf, Woman, and Sun

Slab- and coil-built stoneware
Glaze and Firing: Brushed porcelain slip,
glaze, oil paint, cone 8 oxidation firing
in an electric kiln

d 23 inches
d 58 centimeters

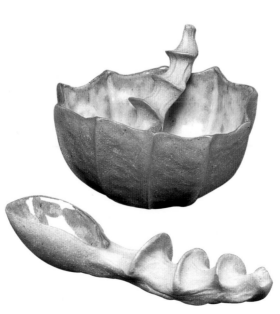

BARBARA WALCH
Bowls and spoons

Pinched and hand-built stoneware
Glaze and Firing: Unglazed exterior,
iron and cobalt blue glazed interior,
cone 10 reduction firing

w 6 × h·2 × d 6 inches
w 15 × h 5 × d 15 centimeters

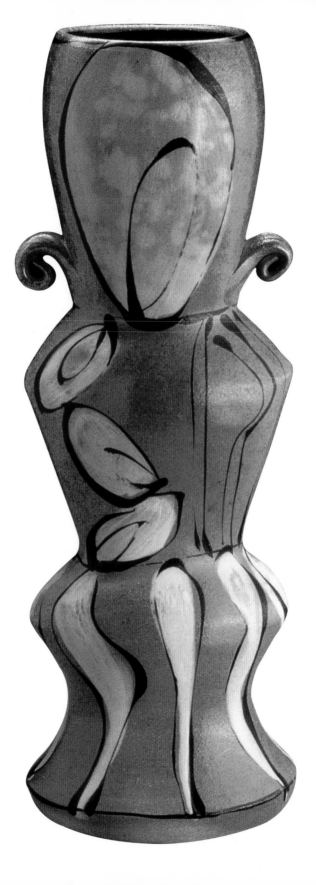

SUZE LINDSAY
Bouquet Vase

Thrown, altered, and stacked stoneware
Glaze and Firing: Slips, cone 10 salt firing

w 3 × h 14 × d 3.5 inches
w 8 × h 36 × d 9 centimeters

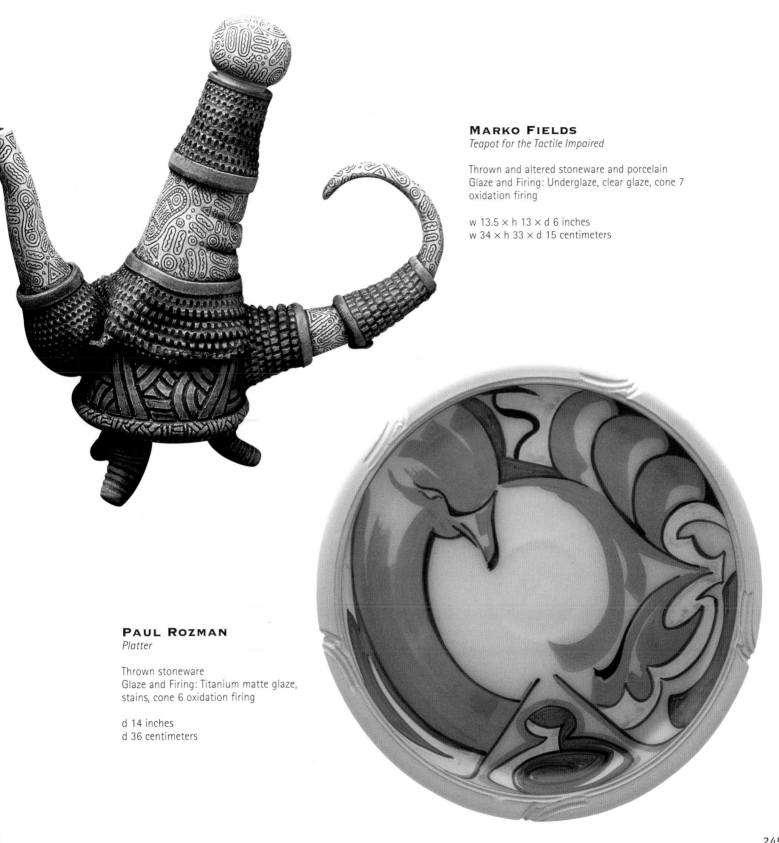

MARKO FIELDS
Teapot for the Tactile Impaired

Thrown and altered stoneware and porcelain
Glaze and Firing: Underglaze, clear glaze, cone 7
oxidation firing

w 13.5 × h 13 × d 6 inches
w 34 × h 33 × d 15 centimeters

PAUL ROZMAN
Platter

Thrown stoneware
Glaze and Firing: Titanium matte glaze,
stains, cone 6 oxidation firing

d 14 inches
d 36 centimeters

PATRICK TUDDY
Salvage-Yard Teapot

Hand-built, slab-built, and press-molded
stoneware
Glaze and Firing: Sprayed glaze, cone 10
reduction firing

w 5 × h 15 × d 24 inches
w 12 × h 38 × d 61 centimeters

BARBARA KNUTSON
Casserole

Hand-built stoneware
Glaze and Firing: Copper/cobalt green glaze,
cobalt green matte glaze, cone 10 reduction
firing

w 9.5 × h 5.5 × d 4.5 inches
w 24 × h 14 × d 11 centimeters

SUSAN O'BRIEN
Sauce boat

Thrown and slab-built stoneware
Glaze and Firing: Cone 10 alkaline and
celadon, lusters, cone 10 soda oxidation
firing/luster firing

w 7 × h 5 × d 4 inches
w 18 × h 13 × d 10 centimeters

BACIA EDELMAN
Lichen Teapot XII

Hand-built stoneware
Glaze and Firing: Layered surfaces, underglazes,
terra sigillata, cone 6 lichen glaze, multi-firing in
an electric kiln

w 14 × h 12.5 × d 4.5 inches
w 36 × h 32 × d 11 centimeters

ROBERT WINOKUR
Pitcher

Slip-cast stoneware from molds
Glaze and Firing: Blue wood ash glaze, slips,
engobes, salt glazes

w 10.75 × h 10.75 × d 5 inches
w 28 × h 28 × d 13 centimeters

CHRIS STALEY
4 cups

Thrown and altered stoneware
Glaze and Firing: Slips, residual salt

w 12 × h 10 × d 12 inches
w 30 × h 25 × d 30 centimeters

LANA WILSON
Ritual teapot

Hand-built stoneware slabs with
hand-made stamps
Glaze and Firing: Layered glazes and engobes,
cone 6 firing in an electric kiln

w 15 × h 8 × d 5 inches
w 38 × h 20 × d 13 centimeters

CHUCK SOLBERG
Ashen jug

Thrown, faceted, and distorted stoneware
Glaze and Firing: Natural ash, four-day
firing in an anagama wood kiln

w 8 × h 12 × d 6 inches
w 20 × h 30 × d 15 centimeters

SANDRA L. LANCE
Nesting Bird Jar

Thrown, altered, modeled, and carved white mid-range stoneware
Glaze and Firing: Underglazes, colored translucent and satin glazes, cone 6 oxidation firing

w 5.25 × h 5 × d 4 inches
w 13 × h 13 × d 10 centimeters

NICKIE MALY AZICRI
Thorn Mother

Hand-built stoneware
Glaze and Firing: Glazes mixed with sand, low-fire firing

w 19.5 × h 18 × d 16 inches
w 50 × h 46 × d 41 centimeters

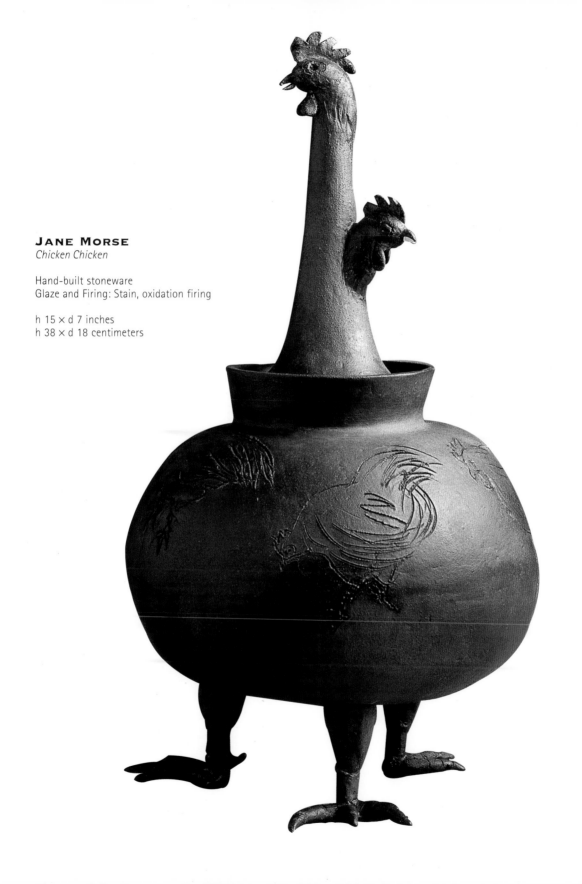

JANE MORSE
Chicken Chicken

Hand-built stoneware
Glaze and Firing: Stain, oxidation firing

h 15 × d 7 inches
h 38 × d 18 centimeters

WALTER DEXTER
Urban Landscape

Hand-built stoneware
Glaze and Firing: Black and white stoneware,
slip, lithium orange glaze, chrome-red glaze,
cone 6 gas and cone 08 multi-firing

w 18 × h 32 × d 4 inches
w 46 × h 81 × d 10 centimeters

MARY BARRINGER
Teapot

Hand-built stoneware
Glaze and Firing: Layered slip, glazes, cone 6
firing in an electric kiln

w 9.5 × h 9.5 × d 4.5 inches
w 24 × h 24 × d 11 centimeters

MARK JOHNSON
Teapot with stripes

Thrown and altered white stoneware
Glaze and Firing: Glazes, wax and latex resists,
cone 10 soda firing

w 10 × h 15 × d 10 inches
w 25 × h 38 × d 25 centimeters

253

JANET HARBOTTLE
Striped Torso

Hand-built stoneware
Glaze and Firing: Layered slips, low-fire glaze,
cone 04 firing in an electric kiln

w 9.5 × h 19.5 × d 7 inches
w 24 × h 50 × d 18 centimeters

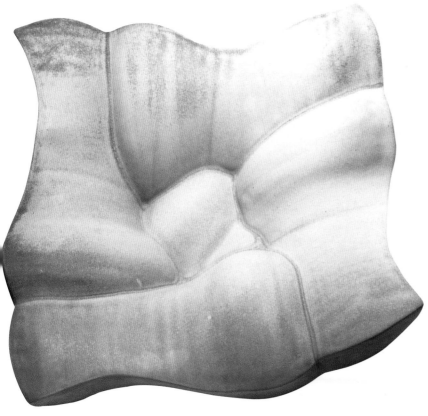

ERICA WURTZ
Dulcet

Thrown and hand-built stoneware
Glaze and Firing: Cone 9 reduction firing

w 14 × h 4 × d 10 inches
w 36 × h 10 × d 25 centimeters

ANN M. TUBBS
Lemons and Blue Wave

Slab-built stoneware
Glaze and Firing: High-fire majolica glaze,
cone 3 and cone 4 oxidation firing in an
electric kiln

w 18 × h 1.75 × d 11 inches
w 46 × h 5 × d 28 centimeters

RAVIT BIRENBOIM
Untitled

Hand-built stoneware on a bisque mold
Glaze and Firing: Henderson glaze,
oxidation firing

w 5–7 × h 2–3 × d 3–4 inches
w 13–18 × h 5–8 × d 8–10 centimeters

MALCOLM E. KUCHARSKI
Covered jar

Thrown and hand-built stoneware
Glaze and Firing: Feldspathic glaze, cone 9
reduction firing

w 24 × h 27 × d 12 inches
w 61 × h 69 × d 30 centimeters

MIKE LEMKE
Window

Thrown, hand-built, and slab-built stoneware
Glaze and Firing: Sprayed and brushed glazes,
low-temperature firing in an electric kiln

w 9 × h 8 inches
w 23 × h 20 centimeters

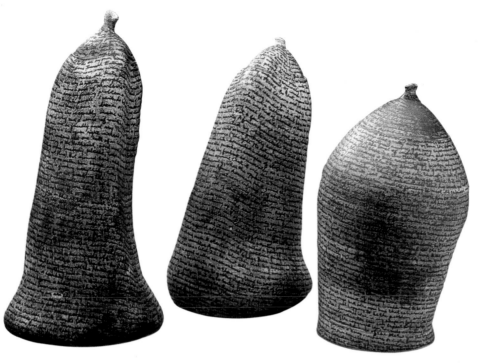

BRUCE A. BARRY
Journal Entry #54, Journal Entry #55, Journal Entry #59

Thrown and altered stoneware
Glaze and Firing: Mason stains, cone 10
reduction glazes, cone 10 reduction firing

h 16, 14.5, 13 inches
h 46, 36, 33 centimeters

SUSAN BEECHER
Tall jar

Thrown stoneware
Glaze and Firing: Wood ash glaze with rutile,
wood firing for 16 hours with salt added

w 7 × h 23 × d 5 inches
w 18 × h 58 × d 13 centimeters

SUSAN EISEN
Vortex

Hand-built, coil-built, and slab-built stoneware
Glaze and Firing: Oxides washes and stains,
cone 10 oxidation firing

w 23 × h 16 × d 17 inches
w 58 × h 41 × d 43 centimeters

INGE GYRITE BALCH
Fossil Fuel environment series #6

Hand-built and assembled stoneware
Glaze and Firing: Oxides, low-fire glazes,
cone 3 and cone 05 firing

w 28 × h 18 × d 7 inches
w 71 × h 46 × d 18 centimeters

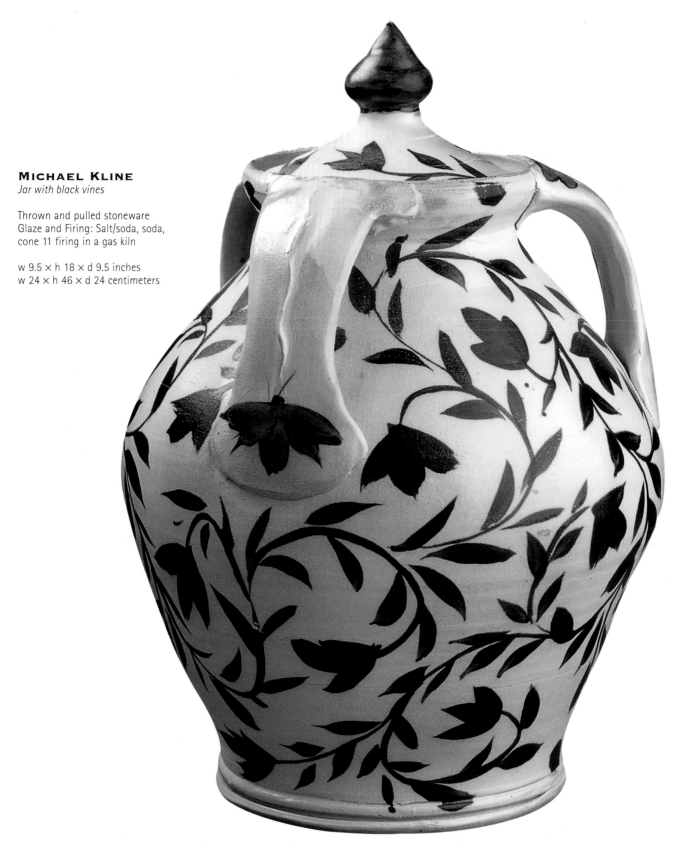

MICHAEL KLINE
Jar with black vines

Thrown and pulled stoneware
Glaze and Firing: Salt/soda, soda,
cone 11 firing in a gas kiln

w 9.5 × h 18 × d 9.5 inches
w 24 × h 46 × d 24 centimeters

MICHAEL COHEN
Two figures guarding vase

Hand- and slab-built stoneware
Glaze and Firing: Black wash, cone 10
reduction firing

w 5 × h 26 × d 7 inches
w 13 × h 66 × d 18 centimeters

MARVIN SWEET
Animistic pitcher

Hand-built stoneware
Glaze and Firing: Poured and
brushed glazes, raku firing

w 12 × h 11 × d 4 inches
w 30 × h 28 × d 10 centimeters

HIROSHI NAKAYAMA
Ceremonial vessel

Thrown, slab-built, altered, and
assembled stoneware
Glaze and Firing: Layered wood ash base glazes,
cone 10 reduction multi-firing

w 12 × h 3 × d 12 inches
w 30 × h 8 × d 30 centimeters

Lori Mills *36, 72*
550 Holley Street
Brockport, NY 14420

Randy Miseph *23*
P. O. Box 467
Falmouth, MA 02541

Nicolette Mitchell *167*
930 Bertrand #1
Manhattan, KS 66502

Hideaki Miyamura *121, 174*
30 Mineral Street
Ipswich, MA 01938

Masako Miyata *135*
P. O. Box 47
Port Republic, VA 24471

Una Mjurka *53*
1266 Shasta Avenue
San Jose, CA 95126-2636

Martin Möhwald *218*
Mesw.2 06114 Halle
Germany

Jerod Morris *99*
840 Dondee
Manhattan, KS 66502

Jane Morse *222, 254*
304 Nettleton Hollow Road
Washington, CT 06793

Judith Motzkin *9, 62*
Judith Motzkin Studio
7 Tufts Street
Cambridge, MA 02139

Edith B. Murphy *191*
501 Randolph Street
Burlington, W.I. 53105
Ediboro, PA 16412

Kevin A. Myers *35, 80*
415 East Dryden
Glendale, CA 91207

Ragnar Naess *202, 235*
North River Pottery
107 Hall Street
Brooklyn, NY 11205-2506

Mark Nafziger *180*
D.B.A. Brush Creek Pottery
300 Stryker Street
Archbold, OH 43502

Hiroshi Nakayama *222, 265*
Fisk Road
Worthington, MA 01098

Charles B. Nalle *109, 162*
P.O. Box 510058
Melbourn Beach, FL 32951

Kathryn E. Narrow *105*
817 North 28th Street
Philadelphia, PA 19130

Mika Negishi *235*
2035 Tecumseh Road
Manhattan, KS 66502

Shannon Nelson *171*
P. O. Box 61468
Fairbanks, AK 99706

Sue Nelson *184*
2347 Ashland Avenue
Santa Monica, CA 90405

Tom Neugebauer *27*
600 Sawkill Road
Milford, PA 18337

Alan Newman *113, 161*
Newman Ceramic Works
4308 Riverdale Road S.
Salem, OR 97302

Brenda Newman *113, 161*
Newman Ceramic Works
4308 Riverdale Road S.
Salem, OR 97302

Mary T. Nicholson *175*
933 Haverstraw Road
Suffern, NY 10901

Richard T. Notkin *211*
P. O. Box 698
Helena, MT 59624

Susan O'Brien *250*
2541 Oleander
Baton Rouge, LA

Jeff Oestreich *220, 241*
36835 Pottery Trace
Taylors Falls, MN 55084

Alena Ort *186*
Alena Ort Ceramics
4 Washington Square Village
New York, NY 10012

Shiro Otani *216*
Kinose 2843-1
Shigaraki-Cho Koka-Gun
Shiga-Ken 529-18
Japan

Kreg Richard Owens *20*
Trinity Clay Productions
312 Sunny Lane
Nampa, ID 83651

Laney K. Oxman *52*
Rt. 9, Hillrose Cottage
Hillsboro, VA 20134-1515

Francine Ozereko *66*
5 Amherst Road
Pelham, MA 01002

Frank Ozereko *73*
5 Amherst Road
Pelham, MA 01002

Marie J. Palluotto *155*
5 Glenview Terrace
Maynard, MA 01754

Shawn Lyn Panepinto *121*
Radcliff College Ceramics
Studio
219 Western Avenue
Boston, MA 02134

Colby Parsons-O'Keefe *113*
189-3 Evergreen Terrace
Carbondale, IL 62901

Neil Patterson *169*
2545 Meredith Street
Philadelphia, PA 19130

Greg Payce *18, 94*
1408 11th Avenue SE
Calgary, Alberta T2G 0Z8
Canada

Angelo di Petta *48*
641 Zion 4th Line
Rural Route 3
Milbrook, Ontario L0A 1G0
Canada

Virginia Piazza *189*
455 Clinton Street
Brooklyn, NY 11231

Robert Piepenburg *51*
24723 Westmoreland
Farmington Hills, MI 48336

Sandi Pierantozzi *55, 84*
2545 Meredith Street
Philadelphia, PA 19130

Grace Pilato *72*
524 S. Allen Street
State College, PA 16801

Frank Pitcher *242*
RR 1, Box 436
Deer Isle, ME 04627

Elizabeth A. Plepis *109*
5 Meetinghouse Road
Hatboro, PA 19040

Paulien Ploeger *215, 266*
Oudebildtdijk 732
9079 NB St. Jacobiparochie
The Netherlands

Rebecca Plummer *206*
Barking Spider Pottery
Box 50
Penland, NC 28765

Sally Porter *34*
5668 Monches Road
Colgate, WI 53017

Sara Post *41*
604 Barbera Place
Davis, CA 95616

Sally Bowen Prange *112*
6421 Heartwood Drive
Chapel Hill, NC 27516

Hunt Prothro *9, 162*
9120 Le Velle Drive
Chevy Chase, MD 20815

Elsa Rady *129, 136, 138*
1500 Andalusia Avenue
Venice, CA 90291

Claudia Reese *36, 74*
Cera-Mix Studios
709 North Tumbleweed Trail
Austin, TX 78733

Don Reitz *223*
P. O. Box 206
Clarkdale, AZ 86324

James G. Robertson *210*
10467 West 8th Plave
Lakewood, CO 80215

Thomas Rohr *149*
4-124 16th Avenue NW
Calgary, AB, Canada
T2M0H2

Elizabeth Roman *109, 140*
Feat of Clay
P. O. Box 161
East Calais, VT 05650

Jerry Rothman *126*
20442 Sun Valley Drive
Laguna Beach, CA 92651

Bill Rowland *217*
1511 Cedar Valley Road
Rural Route 1, Frazierville
Ontario
Canada

Kathleen M. Royster *180*
Box 1262
Salt Lake City, UT 84110

Paul Rozman *47, 248*
106 3219-56th Street NE
Calgary, Alberta T17 3R3
Canada

Harvey Sadow *64, 213*
9540 Quail Trail
Jupiter, FL 33478

Judith Salomon *35, 57*
3448 Lynnfield Road
Cleveland, OH 44122

Steffanie Samuels *199, 246*
829 Tappan Studio 004
Ann Arbor, MI 48104

Robert Sanderson *214*
Cowden Cottage
Abercairny, Crieff
Perthshire, PH7 3QZ
Scotland, United Kingdom

Patricia Sannit *181*
Patricia Sannit Ceramics
1507 Ada Street
Berkeley, CA 94703

Anne Schiesel-Harris *84, 118*
Ash Works
P. O. Box 275
West Park, NY 12493

Judith Schumacher *42*
153 Arbor Court
Boshry Ridge, NJ 07920

Brad Schwieger *191, 194, 234*
13350 Scatter Ridge Road
Athens, OH 45701

Barbara Sebastian *139*
1777 Yosemite Avenue
Suite 4B-1
San Francisco, CA 94124

Bonnie Seeman *166*
9433 Chelsea Drive South
Plantation, FL 33324

Carol Selfridge *48*
9844-88 Avenue
Edmonton, Alberta T6E 2R3
Canada

Richard Selfridge *48*
9844-88 Avenue
Edmonton, Alberta T6E 2R3
Canada

Carol Sevick *117*
Rural Route 3, Box 748
Putney, VT 05346

Mary Kelton Seyfarth *37*
1442 Forest Avenue
Highland Park, IL 60035

Ellen Shankin *218*
Route 3, Box 154A
Floyd, VA 24091

Jeff Shapiro *193*
62 Raycliff Drive
Accord, NY 12404

Kathryn Sharbaugh *106, 152*
4304 Grange Hall Road
Holly, MI 48442

Danny Sheu *207*
125 Gifford Avenue #3
San Jose, CA 95110